More Prais ...
PRAYING IN THE MESSINESS OF LIFE

Be on guard! *Praying in the Messiness of Life* may convince you that a relationship with God is not only possible in our messy world, but it may become the most important reality in your life. A refreshingly written and deeply insightful book you will not want to miss reading!

—E. Glenn Hinson
senior professor of church history and spirituality
Baptist Seminary of Kentucky

Linda Douty generously and honestly shares her own journey with prayer as she addresses a wide range of prayer forms. She provides an incentive for each of us to move beyond worn-out ways and to explore new directions.

With a clear understanding that prayer is a relationship with God, not a routine or ritual, we sense an invitation to grow in grace and intimacy with our loving Creator made known in Jesus and now alive through the Holy Spirit.

Linda Douty's experience as a person of prayer and wise spiritual director shines through these pages which offer clear, practical guidance.

—the Reverend Elizabeth Canham
Episcopal priest and author

PRAYING in the MESSINESS of LIFE

7 ways to renew your
relationship with God

LINDA DOUTY

UPPER
ROOM BOOKS®
NASHVILLE

PRAYING IN THE MESSINESS OF LIFE
7 Ways to Renew Your Relationship with God
Copyright © 2011 by Linda Douty

The Upper Room® Web site http://www.upperroom.org

UPPER ROOM®, UPPER ROOM BOOKS® and design logos are trademarks owned by The Upper Room®, a Ministry of GBOD®, Nashville, Tennessee. All rights reserved.

Scripture quotations not otherwise noted are from the New Revised Standard Version Bible, copyright © 1989 National Council of the Churches of Christ in the United States of America. Used by permission. All rights reserved.
Scripture quotations marked (NIV) are taken from the Holy Bible, New International Version®, NIV®. Copyright © 1973, 1978, 1984 by Biblica, Inc.™ Used by permission of Zondervan. All rights reserved worldwide. www.zondervan.com

"Praying with the Silence" is adapted from Linda Douty, "Silence as Friend, Not Enemy" in *Rhythm and Fire*, edited by Jerry P. Haas and Cynthia Langston Kirk © 2008. Used by permission of Upper Room Books.

The Pattern of Our Days: Worship in the Celtic Tradition from the Iona Community, by the Iona Community, edited by Kathy Galloway, copyright © 1996 by The Authors. Paulist Press, Inc., Mahwah, NJ. Reprinted by permission of Paulist Press, Inc.

"Breathing Compassion" © 2009, "Mindful Walk" © 2007, and "Prodigal Prayer" © 2010 by Steve Garnaas-Holmes are used by permission. unfoldinglight@hotmail.com.

At the time of publication all Web sites referenced in this book were valid. However, due to the fluid nature of the Internet some addresses may have changed or the content may no longer be relevant.
Cover and interior design: Bruce DeRoos / Left Coast Design
Cover photo: © Rafal Olkis / Shutterstock.com
Typesetting: PerfecType / Nashville, TN
First printing: 2011

                    Library of Congress Cataloging in Publication
Douty, Linda.
  Praying in the messiness of life : 7 ways to renew your relationship with
God / Linda Douty.
       p. cm.
  Includes bibliographical references.
  ISBN 978-0-8358-1041-8
  1. Spiritual life—Christianity. 2. Prayer—Christianity. I. Title.
  BV4527.D69 2011
  248.3'2—dc22   2010045442

Printed in the United States of America

To the Academy for Spiritual Formation,

where I learned to pray more deeply

both in the pew and in the pace of life.

CONTENTS

ACKNOWLEDGMENTS

If you have ever written anything, you remember moments when you become so immersed in the material that clarity becomes clouded and the whole manuscript gets garbled in the brain. That's when you need fresh eyes to spot misplaced commas, unparallel structure, and faulty logic. It also helps if the people with those eyes have a box of sharpened red pencils.

So thanks to my quartet of readers—Eyleen Farmer, Anita Fletcher, Brad Thomas, and Suzanne Henley. You saved me from my personal writing quirks and natural preachiness in countless paragraphs. And I say thank you, thank you, thank you.

I'm not one of those folks who can write creatively in small segments in my own home. The phone rings, the laundry needs laundering, and I can't resist checking my e-mail just one more time. My writing self needs to disappear from the world for a few days to allow new thoughts to emerge. Thanks to those of you who provided exquisite writing venues where I could do just that. Freida Pearson and Scottie Brafford: time spent in your lakeside cottages was both renewing and inspiring. Your generosity gave me a place to stare out the window long enough to get in touch with the quiet voice inside that can speak the right words.

It's difficult to adequately express my debt to those courageous individuals who share their stories with me in spiritual guidance sessions. You have enlarged my heart and expanded my grasp of how lovingly the Holy Spirit seeks to shape our lives. Thank you for allowing me to use many of your insights and experiences in this book.

Special thanks go to my editor and friend Robin Pippin and all the folks at Upper Room Books. Your professional expertise and consistent encouragement made the writing process a creative collaboration. Special thanks go to Jeannie Crawford-Lee, who is not only a wizard with words but an editor with deep insight and a wise heart.

And to you, dear friends and family, thank you for encouraging me to put yet one more word on the page. You pulled me out of many ditches of despondence and helped me believe this book could happen.

PREFACE

I'm not sure when I began to feel boxed in by my prayer life. The boundaries began to blur. The formulas faded. My prayer notebook, which had recorded petitions offered and answered, was banished forever to an attic box of outworn relics. My mind wandered during church prayers, and my morning rituals were as dull as dirt. Though I still valued private prayer time, the traditional prayer liturgies in church, and the habitual grace before meals, wasn't there something *more*?

It began as a kind of spiritual squirming, a discomfort that I first judged as rebellion on my part. Inside, I assumed God would not be pleased. However, when my spiritual director encouraged me to view the restlessness not as condemnation but as invitation from God, I was finally able to regard the feeling as a kind of divine discontent. Maybe it was actually a gift—some new growing edge of faith toward which God was nudging me. If we're never led to be uncomfortable with the status quo, we'll never change anything. God is always in the business of inviting us to deeper growth.

There wasn't just one cause of this feeling of disconnection. It was a slow piling up of inconsistencies toward a tipping point where my carefully constructed understanding of prayer began to strain at the seams. OK, then, I told myself. I'll just launch off on a new prayer path. But what kind?

So another threshold was crossed in my spiritual journey. But this time I wasn't sure what was on the other side. If my old ways of praying seemed out of touch with my crazy life, then what was I to do? It was as if I were being invited to connect the dots between the aspirations of my prayer life and the moments of my minute-to-minute life. How could I get them to feel like *one life?*

I tackled the dilemma in the customary way I approach problems: I tried harder to figure it out. I began the practice of Centering Prayer; I got up earlier to pray for others; I bought a new prayer journal. And once again, I became aware of the frustration that comes from trying to micromanage my spiritual life. Though I knew (in my head) that growth in the spirit is more about allowing than controlling, it was hard to let go of my well-developed control mode. I had simply created another "prayer box."

The first thing I had to do was take my hands off the steering wheel and ask for divine inspiration and help. The second thing was to *watch and pray*, not easy for an impatient person. For a time I felt a bit rudderless— without a proper map to the next location. Then one day on my daily walk, I began to pray in a new way. My body joined in, my senses spiked, and I began to play with the possibilities of a deeper awareness of God's presence. Those exploratory wanderings were the beginnings of the new paths and practices that resulted in this book.

A variety of triggers can spark a change in our prayer lives. Often our prayer practices are sabotaged by life itself. Circumstances don't always conform to our agendas, and reliable routines are rendered impossible for a time.

- A colicky baby has us pacing the floor at 5:00 AM, eclipsing morning devotions.
- An elderly parent becomes ill and caretaking sucks up every spare moment.
- An unexpected move to a new city scatters the schedule to the wind.
- Financial constraints force us to work longer hours to make ends meet.

Whatever the cause, life can change in an instant or by inches, and our prayers fall prey to the current calendar. Sometimes the uproar is internal rather than external. Old ways of praying feel contrived, unnatural, like borrowed clothes that don't quite fit. Or maybe we succumb to the harsh reality that our fervent prayers do not yield the result we desire, that putting a coin in the "prayer slot" doesn't always ensure getting the prize we expect. In those piercing moments, we realize that prayer is more mysterious than we thought, less malleable to our manipulation. If we can't figure out the right formula, then what are we to do?

In my work as a spiritual director, I've heard many folks wrestle with these issues. Spiritual direction is actually the work of companionship, of listening prayerfully to the movement of the Spirit in a person's life. It's a privilege to accompany others as they seek to relate more consciously to the spiritual dimension of their lives, and believe me, I learn much more from them than they do from me.

Many have expressed an ongoing sense of guilt, an unspoken frustration that they "can't find enough time for God" or "don't pray enough." The guilt carries many verbal tags, such as:

- Why do I procrastinate about my devotional time?
- Why did I tell Steve I would pray for him and then forget to do it?
- Why does my prayer time feel like one more thing to check off my to-do list?

We can attend retreats, enroll in Bible studies, pray in prayer circles, and read all the latest spiritual books but still find ourselves harried, hurried, and hopping from one thought to the next like nervous rabbits. And this unconscious stress becomes the very air we breathe. It isn't just our own thoughts that jerk us around, of course. This technological age bombards us with more information than we can absorb and more noisy input than our spirits can endure. We lose our center in a swirl of stimulation coming from computers, cell phones, television, and talk radio.

This book won't be about finding more efficient ways to "pray right" so that we can get what we ask for. Instead, it is about developing a friendship with a Friend who won't abandon us no matter how badly we mess up. It's about existing in that friendship—swimming in it, floating in it—rather than trying to manipulate or deserve it. After all, *prayer is really more about relationship than results.*

If any of these wondering, wandering places in the journey of prayer sound familiar, then this book is for you. We'll explore seven ways to renew our relationship with God, to become more aware of God's presence in life *as it is* rather than that mythical day when *things settle down.* We'll discover practices that actually embody that intention, helping us integrate Spirit into the moments of delight and despair, celebration and chaos, contentment and confusion. These practices are grouped into seven clusters: Body, Breath, Mind, Senses, Silence, Surroundings, and Circumstances. Taken together, these can lead us into the possibility of praying with our lives. The suggestions in this book are not meant as prescriptions to heal an ailing prayer life. Rather, they form a buffet of choices designed to move prayer from the margins of the mind into the messiness of life.

It's exciting to explore the limitless boundaries of integrated prayer, as we grow toward practices in which prayer blends with life. Deep inside my own soul lies the comforting belief that *God is more interested in our growth than our guilt.*

Linda Douty

Introduction

BREAKING OUT OF THE PRAYER BOX

I am about to do a new thing;
now it springs forth, do you not perceive it?
ISAIAH 43:19

When I was a child, I spoke like a child, I thought like a child, I reasoned
like a child; when I became an adult, I put an end to childish ways.
1 CORINTHIANS 13:11

She was ten minutes late for her spiritual direction appointment, and the upstairs climb to my office had left her breathless. Christina plopped down in the chair, exclaiming, "Sorry I'm late, but there *never* seems to be enough time anymore!"

After our customary lighting of the candle and opening prayer, she was still in a state of frustration. The agitation came spilling out before I even had a chance to ask her about the state of her soul.

"I planned to start getting up fifteen minutes earlier so I could have more time for God," she began, "but I keep hitting the snooze button instead, just trying to grab a few more moments of sleep, The baby's been colicky and John's feeling some strain at the office, and besides that, the big project I've been working on is almost due! When am I ever going to get back to my regular devotional time?" Besides being exhausted, she was drowning in guilt.

Christina settled back in her chair and took a deep breath, exhaling at least a little of her anxiety. As we prayed and talked about the situation together, we were led from the pious to the practical. Picking up pen and paper, we took an imaginary trip through one of her "normal" days. She was right—there was hardly one uncommitted moment.

But another reality surfaced, one that moved her to gratitude. Her challenging job, her robust family of three children and a loving husband, even her position as the only child of aging, ailing parents—all were stunning gifts of life that she treasured. Her eyes brightened as she admitted, "I'm deeply grateful for all those blessings; I don't want to relinquish a single one of them!"

On the other hand, she was tired of her own futile attempts to find more time to pray, to be "more spiritual." Her pattern of promises to herself had a common thread: various versions of "When This Is Over . . ."

- when the project is completed
- when the bills are paid
- when Mom recovers from the broken hip
- when I retire
- when the kids go to college
- when I have more time
- when my life settles down

In other words, she was busy planning to pray, not praying; she was preparing to live, not living. Though she believed that God can use everything in our lives to shape us and deepen our faith, she felt bewildered about where God might be leading her in this particular dilemma. What spiritual lesson was offering itself to her? In her head, she believed that life is indeed a school of the soul, one from which we never graduate. She knew that everything that happens provides "grist for the mill" in her own spiritual formation process. But how could that concept find its way into the current chaos?

As Christina affirmed the blessedness of her life, it became clear that she was being invited to become more aware of God's presence in her life as it was, at that moment, in the present. Logic told us both that her life never remains the same for very long. Circumstances shift; situations resolve themselves; change would always be a constant reality. So how could she nurture her relationship with God in the midst of unpredictable days?

A comforting sense of God's acceptance began to creep into the conversation that day, and a profound truth started to emerge. We realized that, as a forgiving Presence in her life, God was inviting her to be more free, more creative in her prayer life. Maybe her busyness was not a choice for which she needed to feel guilty but a temporary condition of life. But the practical questions were still hanging: *How can I open myself to growth in this crazy, busy life? What can I actually do, rather than constantly wishing it would change?*

Christina was ready to draw a halt to the mental hand-wringing that plagued her every day, that feeling of not getting it right. She was ready to explore integrated prayer—prayer in the midst of life, not in spite of life. Our discussion led us once again through an exploration of her typical day—hour-by-hour, task-by-task—from the moment she awakened until she closed her eyes at night. In doing so, we discovered that, though the activity appeared to be nonstop, she had significant chunks of time alone in her car—a lengthy commute to her office, trips to school and soccer games and music lessons, attending to her parents' needs. As acceptance of the situation filled her mind, her guilt began to melt away. It was as if the words of Saint Paul took residence in her heart:

> Pray without ceasing, give thanks in all circumstances; for this is the will of God in Christ Jesus for you.
>
> *1 Thessalonians 5:17-18*

THE ROLLING SANCTUARY PRAYER

Paul's admonition was not meant to justify remaining in unhealthy situations that need to change but accepting life circumstances that can't be changed. A miracle began to unfold. As Christina's guilt and anxiety went out the door, a burst of creativity rushed in to take their place. With a playful spirit, she christened her station wagon the Rolling Sanctuary.

Of course, there were ground rules for this unusual spiritual practice in her car. Christina allowed herself no cell-phone conversations except for emergencies, no radio, no snacking, and as little extraneous noise as possible. Over time, with God's grace and guidance, that hunk of metal became a holy enclosure, an outer rolling sanctuary that connected to her inner sanctuary, where her prayers began to flourish.

Her imagination had fun with it! An organized, intentional person by nature, Christina developed a loose structure for her time on the road by using the environment to guide her prayers. You can try her system of rolling sanctuary prayer, adapting it to your own circumstances.

- *At each stop sign*, pray for those who are ill or in special need.
- *At each red light*, pray for the upcoming activities of the day.
- *At each green light*, pray for the flow of love and peace in your own life; may it move powerfully through you to others.
- *When stopped at a train crossing*, use each passing railcar to list things for which you are thankful—one blessing per car.
- *When you notice someone in distress*, breathe a prayer for well-being.
- *When something catches your eye*, allow the visual cue to prompt special prayers. For instance, a pond or a lake might evoke a prayer of thanksgiving for your baptism; a field of flowers may bring spontaneous appreciation of the beauty of creation or the miracle of growth; mile markers, such as "Cincinnati—100 miles," might remind you of a friend living there who needs your prayers or a phone call.

A GROWN-UP PRAYER LIFE

Christina's experience prompted me to think more about the ways God leads us to grow up in our approach to prayer. Just as we mature in our ideas of life and love, our maturing spirituality should involve a deeper experience of prayer. We are told in Luke 2:52 that "Jesus increased in wisdom and in years, and in divine and human favor." Aren't we called to do the same? What would it mean to "grow up" in our prayer life, to allow the Spirit of God to spill over the edges of any box we put it in? Christina's story nudged me to examine my own prayer posture more thoughtfully.

I began to consider the nature of integrated prayer—not simply making more time for prayer as a separate compartment, valuable as that is, but threading my life with prayer, infusing it with a sense of the sacred. Granted, most of us start our sacred journeys trying to "get it right for God" or measure up to some perceived spiritual standard, but that need not be where we end up.

At this juncture the usual path of change—trying harder—didn't seem to fit the invitation to spiritual growth for me. Though it felt uncertain and uncomfortable, this particular stage of my spiritual journey seemed to be more about letting go than trying harder, more about learning to listen to God than telling God what to do, more about inviting God to work with me and through me than redoubling my efforts to curry God's favor and rewards.

It's no easy task to let go and let God, but deeper growth begins at the end of our effort. We are always being invited to lean into our spiritual growing edge, venturing beyond our comfort zone. Wendell Berry said it briefly and powerfully:

> It may be that when we no longer know what to do we have come to our real work and that when we no longer know which way to go we have begun our real journey. The mind that is not baffled is not employed. The impeded stream is the one that sings.[1]

Scripture and history give us countless examples of inspiration that comes at the end of our striving. Saint Paul reached the emptiness of his forced piety, which paved the way for a face-to-face encounter with the blinding Light. When John Wesley released his legalistic agenda for goodness, he felt his "heart strangely warmed."

We enter another stage of growth when we let go of what we can do for God or get from God and enter the mysterious process of what God can do through us and in us. And we may be called to enter an expanded experience of what prayer can be. Just as the verse in Isaiah reminds us, we need to be open to a "new thing," even in our prayer life. For instance, if prayer still consists of one-sided conversations controlled by us, it is woefully incomplete, not to mention boring. It's like having toast and coffee every day for breakfast for forty years.

I can't help wanting to articulate a definition of prayer, though it's doomed from the start. Even the expansive concept of "loving attention to God" feels too limiting, as if I'm trying to contain something in human language that defies containment. So perhaps the only honest thing I can do is share some of my own journey with prayer, hoping it will put you in touch with your journey. Rather than searching for the truth about prayer, or the correct definition—mine or yours—it's more realistic to affirm that our journey of prayer is like any other journey: It doesn't stay the same. It's unpredictable; nothing goes according to our projected plan; we get lost, frustrated, tired, bewildered. If the living Spirit of God, to which we pray as Christians, is indeed *living*, what does that imply? To start with, it means alive, pulsating, changing, evolving, regrouping, growing, expanding. To be alive in the living God is to change and grow, even in our prayer life.

I have never been much on pat answers. For as long as I can remember, I have prayed—sometimes with blind faith and great confidence and sometimes with a mere sliver of hope. At times my faith in prayer would come crumbling down like a house of cards, and my doubts would spiral out of control. I hope that the old adage "Doubt is the cutting edge of faith" is true, because those times of deepest doubt have nearly always wrestled me into greater groundedness.

The searching and questioning have unsettled the soil of my soul, sort of like the springtime process of unsettling the serenity of the garden. I grab a hoe and loosen the dirt so sun and rain can probe to the roots below. Sometimes, faced with the need to till my "prayer garden," all I can say is that I'm willing to "pick up the hoe"—just willing to begin.

Our "prayer garden" can use regular tilling, examination, and cultivation, so that new growth will emerge from outworn assumptions. For instance, we tend to confuse God with Santa Claus. We think that prayer means providing a list of things we want and hoping we have been good enough girls and boys to deserve them. When our prayers are not "answered," we wonder what went wrong. Is there something wrong with us? Were our prayers not fervent enough, our promised changes not enough of a sacrifice? Are we not good enough people for God to heed our prayers?

Or is there something wrong with God? Why is God not moved by our desperate plight and honest pleading? Why won't God give us what we see other people get, especially when we judge them as less deserving than we are?

I remember a heartbreaking example of this way of thinking. A dear friend's young husband was dying of an aggressive form of cancer. Prayer groups and devout individuals all over the city were praying for him, and his faithful wife was convinced that God was healing him. As his condition continued to worsen, she phoned me, saying, "Linda, he's not getting any better. I *must* be praying wrong. Somehow I've got to get it right."

Her sense of guilt and self-judgment not only broke my heart but made me realize how we malign the character of God by implying, however innocently, that God is waiting for us to spout the proper prayer formula before divine healing is released. Not that I have the answer to the secret of healing, mind you, but I know that the God we worship is not a capricious entity to be controlled by us.

It's no wonder we try to manipulate this awesome divine power. That's a familiar prayer box for all of us. In this culture, we're used to getting results from manipulation. We live in a push-button, microwave society. A two-ton automobile can be made to do what we want by the turn of a key. The power of electricity can be tamed to do our bidding. Once we know which icon to click on our computer, we can connect with the world.

Not only can prayer not be manipulated, it can't be measured either, though it's tempting to try. Some years ago, prayer journals were popular, particularly in my part of the Bible Belt. In this kind of journal one kept a record of the content of prayers, then noted the date and time when a prayer was "answered." Religious friends told me, "God always answers our prayers, but sometimes the answer is no." That line of thinking implies that we should not feel sad when things turn out wrong for us, because God wanted it to happen that way. The statement *Prayer works* also bothers me. It always causes a lump in my throat, a silent protest that shouts, "According to whose measuring stick? What about the person who doesn't get the outcome he wants?" The implication is that if we get it right, we can control the outcome of events by manipulating God's will. Maybe to say prayer works really means that we trust God to be with us in a profound and sustaining way, regardless of how things turn out. Though I don't know the answers to the mystery of prayer, I know that my faith in God cannot be dependent on getting the answers I want.

Most of us cut our spiritual teeth on "gimme" prayers, petitions heavy on the asking and light on the receiving. They were usually prayers defined by talking and not listening, seeking God's stamp of approval on what we thought best. In the pages ahead, I invite you to join me in a free-flowing adventure in prayer, one in which we move fearlessly into the Spirit's creative guidance so that our very lives become an embodiment of God's prayer in and through us. I'll say it one more time: prayer is more about relationship than results. It's about loosening our grip on what we *think* we know about prayer and stretching that horizon until we can't see the end of it.

PRAYER AS RELATIONSHIP WITH GOD

This book is an invitation to renew your relationship with God by expanding your prayer experience to include silence as the language of God. We will explore ways to connect with the divine when life has us on the go. We continue to turn to our traditional pillars of prayer: fixed-hour prayer, liturgical prayer, intercessory prayer, prayers offered in community with kindred spirits. We count on these foundational ways of praying for ongoing support and sustenance. But the power of prayer spills over the edges of those boxes too.

Prayer reminds us that we live in two worlds—the world of the senses and the world of mystery. By building bridges between these two universes, prayer helps us to keep the two connected. Moreover, our faith reminds us that in a relationship, someone is on the other end. Somehow someone hears. Steve Garnaas-Holmes captured God's loving listening with these affirming words:

> As you sit in prayer
> and try to remain mindful of God,
> failing because your thoughts wander,
> remember this:
> that God is perfectly mindful of you always,
> attentive to your being and your doing,
> never straying from your heart,
> not missing a single breath,
> or forgetting a single heartbeat.
> God is never distracted, never forgets.
> Without neglecting anything else in Creation,
> for all of Creation is present in God,
> God is fully present to you,
> seeing not from afar but from within
> your journeys, thoughts and feelings,
> holding tenderly your sins and wounds,

delighting in your gifts and beauties,
fully aware of what you yourself
only dimly suspect deep within you.
God is in all that you see, and in your seeing,
in what you hear, and in your hearing,
in your wondering, in your sorrow, in your awe.
God is grateful for you, and delights in you.
God longs in you, grieves in you, exults in you.
God gives full, peaceful, loving attention to you
all your day and all through the night,
not controlling or manipulating,
just beholding, blessing, loving
and breathing life into you,
powerful, joyful, beautiful, infinite life,
granting you mindfulness
and mindful always of you.[2]

FOR REFLECTION

1. How did you pray as a child? How have your ways of praying changed as you've grown up?
2. Do you have special times for prayer? Is your prayer life compartmentalized in "boxes"?
3. What is your favorite excuse for not praying?
4. What current prayer practices are most meaningful to you?
5. What forms of prayer invite you to listen instead of talk?

1

Praying with the Body

Do you not know that your body is a temple of the Holy Spirit within you, which you have from God. . . . therefore glorify God in your body.
1 CORINTHIANS 6:19-20

The body remembers things. Sometimes the muscles store information even when our brains forget it.

My own body rescued me in a senior moment not long ago. I was standing in front of the ATM desperately in need of cash on a day when the banks were closed. When the screen prompt requested my PIN number, I froze. My mind was completely blank, even though I had had the same PIN number for at least ten years. I squeezed my forehead in concentration and tried again. The card came spitting out a second time. I flipped through my mental filing cabinet in search of the numbers; no dice. The harder I tried, the more it eluded me. On the third or fourth attempt, I once again inserted the card, took a deep relaxing breath, closed my eyes, and led with my fingers. Like something on automatic pilot, they instinctively traced the familiar path of the four numbers on the keypad, and soon I had five twenties in my hand. My fingers bore a wisdom of their own.

Remember the tedium of your first bike ride? the painstaking concentration of willing each muscle to maintain the balance? the panic of wondering how to put on the brakes? the scraped knees? Yet, one fine day, your muscles performed their magic with no input from your mind, and from that day on, your body knew how to ride. Muscle memory is a remarkable phenomenon.

Not only does the body remember, it speaks too, sometimes quite clearly. Recently I entered my spiritual direction room to meet with a directee and immediately noticed blinking signs of anxiety. His crossed leg was swinging rhythmically. His eyes were darting from one object to another. His hands clenched, then unclenched. Yet his response to my "How are you?" was the predictable, "Oh, I'm just *fine!*" Sometimes our body language shouts its messages over the din of our empty words, whether we like it or not.

The body communicates in a primal language that we have neglected to learn. In addition, we don't seem to know how to translate its signals into tools for our spiritual growth. With the click of the TV remote or the opening of a newspaper, through a variety of voices and venues, we hear the same message: we are a marvelous matrix of body, mind, and spirit. In fact, the cross communication is so complex that what we think affects what we feel, which affects what we do, which affects our relationships, all of which affect the delicate immune system that manages our health.

Medical studies are affirming this interconnectedness and warning us that we ignore the body's wisdom at our peril. The evidence abounds: anxiety may produce a tension headache; fear causes the heart to race; embarrassment is reflected in a scarlet blush. What would happen if we allowed the body to be an ally in our prayers as well as our health?

Most of us live our spiritual lives in the prayer box called the intellect: reading, studying, analyzing, discussing, hearing sermons, listening to lectures, all of which are commendable. We live with an unconscious disconnect from our bodies, ignoring the guidance of God communicated through this incredible creation. Many of us grew up with the caution that the body was not to be trusted. "If it feels good, do it!" was judged as the mantra of wanton, immoral people. Unfortunately, we were warned that our physical and emotional feelings would betray us and lead us astray. Can we misread the body's urges? You bet. Can we misinterpret the physical communication of others? For sure. But to disregard the body's messages is to devalue God's remarkable gift of the body.

Many of the traditions and rites of the church are physical acts of devotion: kneeling in confession, bowing our heads in prayer, genuflecting, making the sign of the cross, anointing the forehead with oil. Even Communion involves taking substances into the body in remembrance of Christ. The witness of saints through the centuries is that the body belongs in our prayers.

Let's explore several ways our body can help us renew our relationship with God.

LABYRINTH

This revival of ancient sacred geometry reminds me of the words of the prophet Jeremiah: "Stand at the crossroads, and look, and ask for the ancient paths, where the good way lies; and walk in it, and find rest for your souls" (Jer. 6:16). Labyrinths are springing up on the floors of churches, in parking lots, on lawns, and in hospitals. They offer an "ancient path" that spans centuries of pilgrims walking their prayers. For medieval Christians, the labyrinth symbolized the path to the holy city of Jerusalem. For modern Christians, it represents a journey to the heart of God.

The labyrinth differs from a maze in that it has only one entrance and one exit, with no tricks or dead ends. You're always on the path and can trust that you won't get lost. When you meet others on the spiral trail, you simply pass each other in respectful silence and keep going.

Though strolling in circles may seem be to a weird way to pray, the practice has served as a meaningful meditative tool for hundreds of years. As a symbol of wholeness, it represents for many the spiral nature of the spiritual journey inward then out again into the world—truly a pathway with a purpose. No wonder this image is currently enjoying such a renaissance among seekers around the world. It offers tranquility to the mind, serenity to the spirit, and freedom for the body to participate in prayer.

Try the following suggestions to frame your labyrinth prayer:

- Remove your shoes and pause at the entrance, praying that God will lead you in your prayer.
- Walk slowly, breathing deeply, and imagine that you are meandering to the center of your soul, where the Spirit speaks to you.
- When you reach the center, have a leisurely "conversation" with God, bringing your cares and concerns, as well as anything you might need to let go of as you leave the center. Or simply rest in the Presence.
- You may choose to bring a particular question or issue for discernment, praying for wisdom and insight when you reach the center.
- Follow the path back out again, unburdened by anything that might impede your steps toward loving service to God and others.

It is often difficult to refrain from judging the labyrinth experience or evaluating the "results." Trust that God will honor your willingness to offer yourself and will use it for your good. Let go of your need to know the effect of this holy walk.

COMPANION WALK

This walk ignites the soul by sparking the imagination. (Remember that invisible friend you spoke to as a child?)

Picture a silent companion who strolls alongside you, perhaps Jesus or an angel or the spirit of a loved one—whatever might feel natural or comforting to you. Imagine a sacred conversation in which you pour out your gratitude for simple delights, as well as the gift of this presence in your life. Be honest about any concerns or frustrations you may be experiencing.

If you can, envision a dialogue in which you listen to the wisdom of the silent companion. You may want to journal about your experience.

Try to refrain from self-judgment if you attempt this imaginative exercise and it falls flat. The first time I called on a silent companion to walk with me, I felt like a kindergartner playing "Let's pretend." Hold your experience lightly and playfully as your prayer container expands.

SYNCOPATED STEPS

This meditation invites you to use your feet as a metronome, creating a rhythmic beat to your walking while the mind recites a sacred phrase. As the body participates in the prayer, the repetition provides a sort of psychic tattoo in the spirit.

As your feet come in contact with the earth, gratefully affirm the divine foundation of your existence. As you place one foot in front of the other with intentional focus on the contact of your soles with the ground, you embody—or symbolize—your soul's encounter with the Ground of Being. Express gratitude to the Creator God for the interaction of nerve and muscle that makes walking possible.

Simple affirmations lend themselves to syncopated steps and become prayers in motion, accenting the rhythm by stepping as indicated:

- *Love, joy,* and *peace* are *mine.*
- I *open* my *heart* to In*fi*nite *Peace.*
- The *ground* of my *being* is the *God* of *Love.*

For the musically inclined, familiar songs or hymns can provide inspiration with a rhythmic beat. Here are some suggestions; consult your own memory bank for songs that are meaningful to you:

"For the Beauty of the Earth"
"Amazing Grace"
"How Firm a Foundation"

"What the World Needs Now Is Love (Sweet Love)"
"Jesus Loves Me"

REVELATION WALK

In this prayer practice, the walker allows a detail that catches the eye to suggest a personal parable. Stroll along at a leisurely pace, focusing intently on your surroundings. Be open to whatever might draw your attention—a spiderweb, a falling leaf, a puddle of raindrops, a dandelion. Stop and spend time with it, letting your imagination flow. For instance, you might notice a tiny green shoot growing proudly through a crack in the sidewalk, reminding you that Life finds a way through hard times, that as living beings we too strive toward the Light with inherent resilience. Or you might pause to notice how a watery puddle mirrors the details of earth and sky. Stay with the object as long as possible, opening yourself to its lesson for you.

SOAKING PRAYER

What about those days when you are completely drained of energy? This prayer requires minimum effort; in fact, that's the point. Just run a tub of warm water and feel free to add a calming scented oil or bath salts. As you sink into the comforting bath, do nothing and think nothing. Simply allow yourself to soak in the unconditional love of God, who understands and accepts your fatigue after a long, strenuous day.

EXERCISE

For most of us, some form of exercise is part of a regimen for healthy living, a way of honoring and tending the body we've been given. So it makes sense to integrate prayer into activity to which we're already committed.

Quite a number of churches offer classes in yoga or tai chi because these physical disciplines do double duty by toning the body as well as preparing it for prayerful meditation. Even in worship, the body can participate through liturgical dance and other interpretive forms of movement, as well as the simple act of kneeling or bowing.

Many runners witness to the fact that their attentiveness to God is heightened as they experience the rhythm of running. Cycling, rowing, repetitive calisthenics—all present opportunities for repetitive chants and prayers. It's a worthwhile challenge to find creative ways to combine prayer with whatever exercise routine is part of your daily round.

Let's not forget the potential for prayer inherent in plain physical work. For centuries, monks have performed their tasks with prayerful attention and pronounced labor to be a holy endeavor. Every day is full of opportunities to infuse daily chores with prayer:

- While making the bed, express gratitude and prayerful support for the person who sleeps there.
- During window cleaning, pray to see more clearly with the eyes of love.
- When repotting a plant, ask what in your life needs a larger container of expression or understanding.
- Even while sweating and straining, be reminded of the amazing wonders of the body.

No part of us is separated from the creative animation of the Spirit.

HANDS

Simple hand movements can deepen the meaning of the following prayer. It is useful in uniting a group in a service endeavor or in creating bonds of friendship and purpose. The leader reads the prayer slowly, asking participants to move their hands in accordance with the prayer's descriptions.

I see, Lord, *in my tightly clasped hands*, the representation of myself.

I hold on to myself—my cares, possessions, pride.

I shut you out, lest you change me.

I shut out other people, lest they would know me, lest they would hurt me.

In fact, with these fists I could strike out against those who would threaten me.

But I can see in my whitened knuckles and tense forearms what this is doing to me!

I am uptight, enslaved, imprisoned with myself.

I am tired, tense, lonely, and am only destroying myself.

And now in *slowly opening my hands*, I release myself to you, Lord.

Take my guilt, cares, burdens, emptiness, and loneliness.

My arms no longer hurt!

My knuckles are no longer white!

Thank you, Lord, for your release, for freedom, for peace.

With open hands I can no longer shut you out, shut out other people, or strike out against those who would threaten me.

Open hands are for helping.

Fill them with your love.

Show them what to do, how to witness, how to serve.

Suddenly I am aware of the hurts and needs of others, of other situations.

In my mind's eye, I place them in these hands and *lift them* to you for your sustaining grace and healing love.

No longer alone, I *reach out to clasp the hands of my brothers and sisters.*

I thank you, Lord, for them.

Shape us together into the body of Christ.

AMEN.

(Anonymous)

By far the most popular form of praying with the hands is the practice of journaling. Writer Madeleine L'Engle called journaling her "free psychiatrist's couch" where she dumped all her emotional garbage and frustrations. Sometimes putting pen to paper can make our prayers more understandable and concrete. Journaling can develop into a powerful conversation with God.

As you ramble on about your issues, deeper thoughts begin to sneak between the lines. Spiritual journaling moves beyond the mere description of life events. Set aside a time to let the yearnings of your heart travel down the arm to the page without passing through the head. This is no time to pay attention to spelling, punctuation, speed, style, or grammar. Instead, clean out the corners of your consciousness—both the trash and the treasures. Journaling provides legible proof that you want to walk and talk with God. It isn't about writing ability; it's about *availability*.

Miraculous as it sounds, we've been created with an extraordinary inner guidance system. When we befriend our body and learn the unique language of this interior system, it can prove to be a remarkable ally in the life of prayer.

FOR REFLECTION

1. How does your body communicate with you when you are under stress—with headache, nausea, fatigue, back pain, tight shoulders, closed throat?

2. How does your body signal its aliveness—smiles, tears, enthusiasm? Describe the precise physical sensations if you can.

3. What is one daily physical activity that you can integrate into your prayer life?

4. Choose the walking meditation that appeals to you. Take several minutes to experience it, preferably outdoors. If that isn't possible, walk around the room, following the instructions as closely as you can. Invite your body to "pray with you."

2

PRAYING WITH THE BREATH

*Then the Lord God formed man from the dust of the ground,
and breathed into his nostrils the breath of life; and the man
became a living being.*

GENESIS 2:7

*Likewise the Spirit helps us in our weakness; for we do not know
how to pray as we ought, but that very Spirit intercedes with sighs
too deep for words.*

ROMANS 8:26

T ake a deep breath and count to ten," my favorite teacher coun-
seled when we stood red-faced and angry on the playground.
She may not have known it, but she was repeating the wisdom
of the ages. One of our most potent prayer partners is literally right under
our noses.

To enlist the aid of the breath, we don't have to read anything, buy
anything, or perfect a complicated skill. We just do what comes naturally,
and pay close attention to it. The breath reminds us that something outside ourselves, yet miraculously inside, is propelling our lives, breathing
in us and through us. It's automatic and always available. No wonder religious traditions around the globe have recognized the power of linking
our prayers with the breath, an instant connection to the kingdom within
each of us that brings us squarely into the present moment. There's no

way to return to a past breath or fast forward to a future one. You're here, now, being breathed by the God of the universe.

The following prayer practices are based on this dependable connection of breath and spirit.

BREATH PRAYER

For centuries, spiritual masters have pointed to the simple practice of attentive breathing, choosing a phrase that calls to God on the inhale and expressing a deep desire on the exhale. The famous Jesus Prayer (*Lord Jesus Christ, have mercy on me, a sinner*) has brought many a saint and sinner closer to divine comfort.

The method is uncomplicated: select a name or metaphor for God that feels right to you for this particular prayer, attaching it to the inhaling action of the breath; formulate a brief phrase expressing your petition, desire, or affirmation and attach it to the exhale. Or you may use a favorite scripture passage or meaningful phrase to shape your prayer. The witness of praying people through the ages is that repetition somehow grooves a neural and muscular pathway in the brain and body, allowing the body to participate in the prayer. When we pray the same breath prayer over a long period of time, just breathing it whenever it occurs to us, the body seems somehow to learn it, allowing the mind to slip into the unconscious realm where the Holy Spirit prays for us "with sighs too deep for words" (Rom. 8:26). Though I'll list some sample prayers here, I urge you to create your own breath prayer from the seat of your soul, as the Spirit guides you.

INHALE	EXHALE
God of Wisdom,	be my guide.
Loving Creator,	I join in your work.
Divine Light,	shine on my path.

Speak, O God,	my heart is open.
The Lord is my Shepherd,	I shall not want.
Those who wait on the Lord	will renew their strength.
God of Power,	your strength upholds me.
O Great Healer,	heal my soul and body.
God of Comfort,	calm my spirit.
Make me a channel	of your love and grace.
God of Love,	minister through me.
I trust you, Lord,	and all is well.

PAUSE PRAYER

The pause created by a deep breath can be your greatest ally in choosing to *respond* rather than *react*. It brings you back to the here and now and allows you to enter the space of guidance.

This prayer involves willingness to notice your emotional baggage and to "own your stuff." The Pause Prayer requires that you listen intently to the messages of the body that you may rarely examine—your everyday, garden-variety emotional surges.

Think of a moment you would describe as an instant of impatience: the tightening of your jaw when the person preceding you in the check-out line can't find her checkbook, the tapping of your fingers on the table when the waiter won't look your way, the exasperated pacing as you wait for the friend who is always late.

Your reliable inner compass constantly signals you with emotional surges and physical cues. You may feel irritation, anger, disgust, impatience, or dislike. Or you sense the adrenaline rush of delight, laughter, joy, or exhilaration.

Rather than rushing to react, the Pause Prayer allows you to access deeper wisdom. Listen to the important information about yourself available through this prayer. When you sense an emotional surge:

○ Take a deep breath.

○ Accept the fact that you are a human being with human responses.

○ Shift to spontaneous thanks for something specific, and watch the energy change.

○ Breathe a benevolent breath of appreciation for whatever has triggered the emotion. If an interruption makes you smile instead of frown, add that to your store of self-knowledge as you learn what gives you a feeling of aliveness.

○ If the emotional surge is negative, rather than rush to judgment of someone else or yourself, ask: *What in me is getting hooked? What wounded part of me just had the scab knocked off and needs my compassion? What fear is being triggered? Is there a way to express my feelings within proper boundaries?*

Thank God for this wise inner guidance system.

RELEASE PRAYER

This practice enables you to release anxiety with an expansive belly breath, letting the steam out of the tension. Begin by cultivating what singers call abdominal breathing, allowing the incoming breath to lift the abdomen, not just the chest cavity. To get the hang of it, lie flat on the bed or floor and consciously expand your abdomen as you inhale, filling your lungs to capacity. Then let your belly fall, pushing all the breath out as you exhale. The chest remains relatively still.

○ As you breathe in deeply, gather all the confusion and chaos you are experiencing into one breath, and breathe it out fully on the exhale, releasing it to God for healing.

○ You can even use the phrases "I breathe in peace; I breathe out anxiety" to capture your intention to release the anxiety.

○ If a specific concern plagues you, something you can't fix, use this release prayer to trust the outcome to God, believing you will receive the strength to deal with whatever results from the situation. Just breathe it *out*.

BEDTIME BREATH PRAYER

Do you ever have trouble settling down for sleep? Your mind races, your body twitches, your heart pumps quickly. And of course your breath keeps pace with all of it. These are sure signals of a sleepless night ahead.

Believe it or not, your breath can come to the rescue and reverse that entire physical sequence. Begin by breathing in to the count of four, holding the breath to the count of four, and exhaling to the count of four— forcing your breathing rate to slow down. Each time you exhale, increase the count by one, all the way up to eight, while maintaining the inhale and holding the breath to the count of four. By lengthening the exhaling breath, all the other body systems tend to slow down.

After a few moments, breathe naturally and evenly and let go of any anxiety by praying these words:

> Breathing in, I calm my body.
> Breathing out, I smile.

You'll find that it's difficult to hold on to anxiety and to smile at the same time. Here are other suggestions for sleep-inducing prayers to attach to your deep breathing:

> Inhale: Breathe on me, Breath of God;
> Exhale: Fill me with life anew.
> Inhale: All shall be well; all shall be well;
> Exhale: All manner of thing shall be well.
>   (Prayer of Julian of Norwich)

Play with this concept and fashion your own bedtime breathing ritual. Who said you couldn't be rocked to sleep with prayer?

PRAYER OF COMPASSION

This is a beautifully crafted prayer written by Rev. Steve Garnaas-Holmes, a United Methodist pastor who authors an e-newsletter available from unfoldinglight@hotmail.com. He captures the unifying concept of the breath in this stunning poem "Breathing Compassion."

Breathe in.
Breathe deeply.
Breathe in love.

It is love, all this that surrounds you,
surrounds you perfectly,
touches you perfectly,
holds you, contains you, fills you perfectly.
You breathe it.
You move through it.
Everything you see, you see through it.

The breath of love
is given, breathed into you,
from lungs divine
that breathe everything,
that have been breathing from all eternity,
breathing the one spirit we all breathe.

There is only One Breath.
Every breath is the one Breath
breathed into the dust
that was taken up from the ground,
and it became a living being.
With every breath, you become a living Being,
a loving being.

Breathe in this love deeply.

Let it fill you,
enliven you,
change you.

And breathe out.[1]

FOR REFLECTION

1. Consider your own "instant of impatience." What does it feel like in your body? In your daily life, what is the most common trigger for this emotional surge?
2. Set aside time to formulate your personal breath prayer. Imagine Jesus standing in front of you, asking you to name your deepest yearning.
3. What would your most honest response be?
4. How might you make this desire into a breath prayer? Be sure it's what your soul really wants, rather than what you think you ought to want.

3

PRAYING WITH THE MIND

*Finally, beloved, whatever is true, whatever is honorable, whatever is just, whatever is pure, whatever is pleasing, whatever is commendable, if there is any excellence and if there is anything worthy of praise, **think about these things.***
PHILIPPIANS 4:8 (emphasis added)

*We destroy arguments and every proud obstacle raised up against the knowledge of God, and we **take every thought captive to obey Christ.***
2 CORINTHIANS 10:4-5 (emphasis added)

I t matters what we think. In fact, science is telling us in study after study that there is no such thing as an idle thought. Just as radio waves or telephone transmissions carry powerful messages, so do the invisible vibrations produced by our thoughts. And they affect us and those around us, for good or ill. In other words, thoughts produce feelings; feelings produce emotions; emotions produce action; action produces experience. Saint Paul's counsel to us seems prophetic: "be transformed by the renewing of your minds" (Rom. 12:2).

However, our culture seems much more obsessed with what we eat than what we think. How many calories? How much fiber? Did we get our five servings of fruits and vegetables today? What we eat is important, of course, but I wish we paid that much attention to what we feed our minds. We take "bites" from a huge buffet of offerings: violent movies, ridiculous TV sitcoms, trashy novels, idle gossip—all junk food for the brain. In order to monitor what our minds "eat," we must become aware of our own complicity in this junk-food diet.

A Native American fable drives this truth home.

> The story goes that an old Cherokee chief was listening to his despondent grandson, who described a battle between two friends on the playground.
>
> The grandfather got a faraway look in his eyes and said, "Yes, I know what you mean, but the *real* battle is somewhere else . . . and it's between two wolves. "
>
> "What do you mean?" questioned the little boy.
>
> The old man replied, "We have a battle raging all the time inside every one of us—where no one else can see. One wolf is negative— he wears anger, envy, jealousy, greed, arrogance, self-pity, resent- ment, false pride, inferiority, superiority, and ego. The other wolf is positive. He wears joy, peace, love, hope, serenity, humility, kindness, generosity, truth, compassion, and faith. It's an ongoing battle. "
>
> "Well," said the grandson, "who wins?"
>
> And the wise old man replied, "Oh . . . the one you feed."[1]

After first hearing this story, I began to notice the subtle (and not-so- subtle) ways that I feed the negative wolf: by repeating a criticism, by call- ing a friend to complain about someone who has slighted me, by engaging in a vengeful fantasy of "if he does that again, here's what I'll say," or better still, "here's what I wish I had said!" Just as life-enhancing emotions grow by being fed, so do the emotions that choke the life from us. To state the obvious: energy flows where attention goes.

Having said that, I must insert a caveat. I'm not suggesting that we stuff our negative emotions down an interior rabbit hole, resulting in an unhealthy suppression of feelings. All emotions are real and need to be acknowledged and examined. What is the anger or bitterness about? Is our judgment an effort to focus on someone else's actions rather than our own? Perhaps calmly confronting a person or standing up for justice would be better responses. Once we examine negative emotions and make a responsible decision, usually we find a way to move on rather than settle down permanently in an unhealthy internal environment.

In this chapter, we will examine several approaches to prayer that shape the mind in a more positive direction. These can prepare our minds for a more honest relationship with God. Experiment with the methods to discover the ones that suit your wiring best.

INTENTIONAL THOUGHT PRAYER

In this prayer discipline you consciously pay attention to the terrain of your own mind. Ask yourself: *What messages am I giving myself? What judgments of others am I rendering? What mind food am I swallowing? When do the words I say not match the thoughts I'm thinking?* Through the intentional thought practice, you invite God to raise your awareness of occasions when you are feeding the negative wolf, or, on the other hand, refusing to acknowledge feelings. You intentionally notice the thoughts, take responsibility for them, let go of justifying them, and choose a better thought. This kind of digging around takes courage and a belief in God's grace and forgiveness, because often the truth can be pretty ugly:

- ○ Sometimes we play nice with people yet make insinuating remarks about them to others. Have you ever said something like "Well, she's OK, I guess, but . . . "?
- ○ Sometimes we spout so much angry venom to others that we probably raise our own blood pressure. We tell yet one more person, "You won't believe what he did!"
- ○ Sometimes we demean others in subtle, self-serving ways to inflate our own sense of worth: "They can do what they want, of course, but *I* do it this way."

This prayer method is simple but not easy. Become a careful monitor of your own thoughts, noticing them not with condemnation but with a grateful release to God, then turning to a more positive thought. Again, the goal is not suppression of feelings but growing self-awareness. However, when you go over the same resentments again and again, those negative neural pathways are deepened. You can become stuck, for instance, in an internal victim stance that slowly becomes part of your identity. Unconsciously, victimhood becomes a badge of honor, a reason to remain stuck, an excuse for not doing the vital work of forgiveness and letting go. Besides, those negative feelings can wreak havoc on both the spirit and the body. It's like drinking hemlock and expecting someone else to get sick.

Unfortunately, no one can monitor your thoughts except you. Pray that God will increase your awareness of your own repetitive negative thoughts, then cooperate with God by replacing them with those of gratitude and abundance. It may be necessary to make a lengthy list of positive statements so that you can refer to them quickly. Here are some examples:

- I am grateful for all that I have and all that I am.
- I am a willing vessel for the love of God.
- In this moment, I surrender to the presence and power of God.
- I move through this day with energy and hope.

This is a challenging discipline, but over time, a new neural pathway can be grooved in the brain, one that serves your spirit and body with positive, healing energy. In our spiritual laziness, we're often guilty of praying that God will intervene and fix things, doing the work of thought monitoring for us. We've been given the gift of free will; God will not arbitrarily take away that which we refuse to release. Having said that, I'll add another caveat. As we take responsibility for our part of this process, we must also remember to move from controlling to allowing, that is, releasing our limiting thoughts to the greater wisdom of God. In other words, the rational mind is the servant, not the master.

PRAYING WITH SCRIPTURE

The ancient Benedictine practice of *lectio divina* (literally, "spiritual reading") can breathe new life into our reading of scripture. In the context of this practice the Bible is not a fixed set of words and images but the living Word of God, which enters our prayer as something dynamic and alive. In her classic book on the spiritual disciplines, Marjorie Thompson's simple translation of the Latin words is helpful.

> There are four basic phases in the classic practice of spiritual reading, termed in Latin *lectio, meditatio, oratio,* and *contemplatio.* For a basic English equivalent, add the letter *n* to each. The ordering of these four phases represents a general and often natural sequence of progression, not to be understood rigidly. In practice we may experience great fluidity between them, a weaving back and forth as the Spirit moves us.[2]

Several years ago, The Upper Room produced reminder cards that simplified the method:

1. READ a biblical passage, savoring key words.
2. REFLECT on what God may be saying to you as you read the passage again.
3. RESPOND by offering your reflection to God in prayer.
4. REST in God's presence, being open to God's word for you.

This time-tested way of reading the Bible encourages us to move toward transformation, rather than just information, in our encounter with holy scripture. Rather than trying to capture scripture, this method allows scripture to capture us.

SCRIPTURE MEMORY VERSE

This simple prayer discipline involves memorizing a brief Bible passage in the morning and carrying it on your heart throughout the day—breathing it, repeating it, probing its message to you. Here are a few suggestions:

○ Isaiah 26:3: "Those of steadfast mind you keep in peace—in peace because they trust in you."
○ Psalm 46:10: "Be still, and know that I am God!"
○ Psalm 23:1: "The LORD is my shepherd, I shall not want."

Choose a passage that conveys special meaning for you. Take a few moments to commit it to memory, reinforcing its message by frequent repetition.

JOURNALING

The time-tested practice of journaling is a discipline of the mind as well as the body (see page 32). Just writing something down often provides immediate relief, especially if we allow the words to move from our minds down the arm to the page without passing by that pesky editor who lives in our heads. Think of journaling as a kind of divine flow chart, with feelings moving from the head to the heart to the paper. In spiritual journaling, the inner critic needs to be fired—you know, the one who says, "That's not a complete sentence. Did you spell that correctly? What will people think if they read this? Surely you don't mean *that*! Are you nuts?"

Over time, a kind of spontaneous conversation develops on the pages. New thoughts bubble up. Solutions and insights appear. God guides us through the unfettered expressions of the soul as we write those longings on paper.

MINDFULNESS

To be mindful is simply to pay attention, to be 100 percent present to what's happening, even if it is scrubbing pots and pans. Across the centuries, the witness of Brother Lawrence, who performed his kitchen duties "to the glory of God" (as recorded in the seventeenth-century text *The Practice of the Presence of God*) continues to remind us that our connection to God can be deepened by almost anything if the task is done mindfully. A humdrum activity can be transformed into a prayer of the heart.[3]

Here are two practices that help us embody these truths. The first is adapted from an essay by Steve Garnaas-Holmes in his online newsletter.

○ *Mindful Walk:* Sometimes you can walk in the woods simply to be mindful. There are other walks, too . . . walks to think about things, walks to maintain the trail. But a mindful walk is just to practice being there. Walk in order to be open to God's Presence. Just pay attention. Notice what you see, what you feel, what you think. As thoughts come to you, let them go, like the bushes that you pass. Simply notice that those thoughts were there and then let them go so that you can pay attention to what is there in you and before you *now*—not a moment ago. You may realize that you are deep in thought and have not really seen where you've been for the last few moments. The trees don't mind. They just welcome you back to the present moment. The more you practice this, the more likely you will be mindful and present all day long. The point is not to be happy; it is to be present.[4]

○ *Mindful Task:* This practice involves taking a specific, simple task and allowing it to trigger your prayer.

1. While dressing each morning, pray to clothe yourself in the grace of God.

2. When washing your face, pray that all falseness will be washed away and your true self will emerge.

3. As your broom sweeps dirt away, allow your heart to be swept clean of resentment.
4. As you tuck your children (or yourself) into bed, express gratitude for life and entrust them to the nurture and care of God.
5. Even as you pay the bills, remind yourself to be thankful for the contribution that others make to your life.

Find creative ways to embrace the activities of your day with mindfulness. In doing so, you get a taste of what it means to "pray without ceasing" (1 Thess. 5:17).

CREATIVITY

As children of a Creator God, we seem hardwired to practice our own unique versions of the creative process. Many gardeners describe their most sacred moments of connection to God as those when they plant and cultivate—participating in the holy process of growth. Weavers weave the threads of their lives in divine harmony as they practice their craft on the loom. Cooks lose themselves in the colors and textures of food, blending them into reminders to "taste and see that the LORD is good" (Ps. 34:8). Photographers report that zooming in on a flower or widening the lens for a landscape opens them to the wonder of creation. Painting, singing, writing, knitting, shaping pottery—all creative activities can be potentially prayerful pursuits.

AFFIRMATIVE PRAYER

The term *creatures of habit* isn't just a catchy phrase. Its truth is gaining credence in the world of science as well as in our everyday world of observation. As noted, each time we engage a thought, a particular neural pattern deepens. The more frequently a behavior or feeling is repeated, the more likely it is to be repeated again. No wonder Christians through the centuries have employed chant, prayer beads, and other forms of repetitive prayer.

Mark 11:24 underscores the need for this kind of prayer: "So I tell you, whatever you ask for in prayer, believe that you have received it, and it will be yours."

State your prayers as affirmations:

- ○ God is my Light and my Salvation (rather than "Be my light . . .").
- ○ The Lord of life walks with me (rather than "Please walk with me").
- ○ Healing Presence, you bring me strength (rather than "Please bring me strength").
- ○ I am a channel of God's loving-kindness (rather than "Help me be a channel . . .").

We are the gatekeepers of our own minds, monitoring what enters and what exits. Though much enters our minds whether we want it or not, we still have a choice about how to deal with that "content." Even in the case of traumatic events, once we give proper attention to feelings and wounds, participating in the healing work of God, we can choose to move on. To oversimplify, however, our minds are like blank chalkboards, and we hold both the chalk and the eraser.

FOR REFLECTION

1. Be an observer of your own mind for a while. What is the customary nature of your thoughts? judgment, self-criticism, complaint, self-pity, self-doubt? spontaneous gratitude? encompassing love?
2. How can you become a better manager of your mind?
3. What are some affirmative thoughts with which you can build new patterns in your mind? Make a personal list for yourself.
4. Select a creative activity that you enjoy (such as gardening, fishing, cooking, knitting, carpentry, photography). How might you infuse that activity with sacred meaning?

4

PRAYING WITH THE SENSES

I praise you, for I am fearfully and wonderfully made.
PSALM 139:14

O taste and see that the LORD is good.
PSALM 34:8

Since I was already *in* a stew, I decided to literally *make* a stew. Upset by some sort of squabble, I was soon chopping, dicing, sniffing, mixing, simmering, stirring my way back to sanity. Losing myself in the colors, aromas, taste, feel, and the chop-chop of the knife became a kind of sensate prayer that brought me to my senses.

Cooking is often a vehicle of prayer for me. As I sort out flavors, adding leftover vegetables from the refrigerator, I try to blend them into some sort of tasty combination, using what I already have. In a surprising alchemy of attention, my thoughts are led to explore how my life can be better blended into balance and harmony, what belongs and what doesn't belong, what adds spice, what ingredients bring a balance of flavors. The kitchen becomes my place of creative personal prayer.

The life-giving properties of our five senses are astounding gifts of the Creator. Why not engage their potential to deepen our prayer lives and our relationship with that Creator? The following practices can lead us in that direction, expanding our expectations of what prayer can be. The first exercise includes all the senses; then we'll explore them one by one.

STROLL FOR YOUR SOUL

Sensory walks invite us to stop and smell the roses—literally. This contemplative stroll takes us out of the realm of the intellect (where so many of us try to live out our spirituality) and allows us to concentrate on the miraculous gifts of the senses.

Go to a quiet, natural environment if possible—perhaps a park, botanical garden, or woodland area. Walk tall, lifting your head and chest with a deepening awareness of how your body feels in motion, allowing your spirits to lift along with your body.

- For several minutes, focus only on what you *hear*—the birds, the rush of the wind, the crackle of leaves beneath your feet.
- Then move to the sense of *touch* as you stop to feel the silkiness of a flower or sift a handful of dirt through your fingers.
- Next, sniff deeply as you become aware of the assortment of *smells* surrounding you.
- Then cast your *eyes* on the beauty in every direction, from colors in the sky to a squirming caterpillar on the path.
- Lastly, open your *mouth* and drink in the taste of the air that you share with all living things. Their emissions into the atmosphere enter your cellular cycle just as your breath enters their environment. Allow natural gratitude to bubble up for your body's capacity to *see, hear, touch, smell, and taste* all these wonders.

SEE

- *Art as Prayer:* Visit a good art museum and feast your eyes on the array of images and colors that have enriched people for centuries.
- *Play with Paints:* Even if you think you aren't an artist, get some paints or crayons or markers and play with the colors. Let yourself experi-

ment. You will be affirming the creative source within you, which connects to the Source of all beauty.

○ *Praying with Color:* If you are a pray-er who is word weary, this prayer form may be for you. My friend and walking pal Sybil MacBeth has written a groundbreaking book titled *Praying in Color*, which is a treat to the eyes as well as the prayer life. A natural doodler, she explains how her doodles morphed into prayers. Better still, she instructs the reader in how to turn mindless activity into mind*ful* activity and pray through the process. The process is simple and suited to individual sensibilities. Assemble colored pens and other art supplies, relax with a scripture, and start doodling a shape—any shape—containing a person's name. Add swirls and designs and colors to express your prayer. Sybil explains that praying in color gives God "a new way to penetrate the locked cells of our own hearts and minds."[1]

○ *Camera as Prayer Tool:* Even an amateur photographer is often awestruck at the sight of a child's face through a zoom lens or the singular focus on a purple iris in bloom. A camera lens can reveal a microcosm of the world's wonder as the eyewitness to intricate design, human emotion, or a simple landscape. Allow your camera to become a channel of prayer as it captures a snow-capped mountain or a single smile.

HEAR

○ *Sounds to Prompt a Prayer:* Be still and listen. Fling a window open and breathe a breath of gratitude for the birds that are singing, the neighbor who is Weed Eating, the planes roaring overhead. Feel your connection to all the sounds you hear.

○ *Music to Move the Soul:* What music brings a lump to your throat or tears to your eyes? What melodies make you jump with joy? What cadences spark the natural rhythms of your body? Anything that reminds you of the wonder of your own created self can trigger a prayer. Whether you are reacting in sadness or joy, the feelings testify to the humanness you share with all people. Music can calm, excite, enliven, and, yes, carry your prayers. So select the music that moves you. Hearing it with loving attention sings a song to your soul.

TOUCH

- *Gardening:* The Bible brims with gardening metaphors. In his parables, Jesus used lilies, seeds, soil, trees, crops, and more to convey characteristics of the kingdom of God. Literally getting your hands in the dirt can put you in touch with elemental creativity and wonder. Let the soil run through your fingers; touch the velvety rose petal, caress the rough bark on the oak tree. Plant a seed, affirming its potential for growth as well as your own!

- *Touch of Skin:* Don't overlook the powerful energy in the touch of someone's skin. Whether you are bathing a baby's satiny skin or enjoying the touch of a lover, the miracle of intimate touch can be a prayerful celebration of God's gift of touch. From the "laying on of hands" and anointing with oil to washing the feet of the disciples, biblical images remind us that intimate touch not only has a healing power but also has prayer power.

- *Pottery:* Though I'm not a potter myself, I've noticed the prayerful look of peace on the faces of those at the potter's wheel. As their hands drip with liquid clay in search of a shape, the lyrics of the hymn "Spirit of the Living God" often come to mind: "Melt me, mold me, fill me, use me." Shaping clay is a tactile reminder that the Spirit of God shapes and transforms us.

SMELL

What images invade your mind when you smell cookies baking? the distinctive aroma of a sandy beach? the fragrance of lilies? When I get a whiff of coconut, I vividly recall my mother patiently grating a raw coconut for Christmas ambrosia and fresh coconut cake, and I remember what hard work it was. Prayers of gratitude for all the sacrifices my mother made for our family naturally arise. Just as the scents can trigger memories, they also can trigger prayers.

○ *Eucharistic Aromas:* The first time I received Holy Communion by intinction (dipping a bit of bread into the cup of juice or wine), I understood why generations of Christians have responded to smells—the smell of incense and candles, and, on this occasion, freshly baked bread. As retreatants entered the sanctuary for daily Eucharist during a session of the Academy for Spiritual Formation, we were greeted with the yeasty aroma of a hot loaf of bread. At the altar, a warm chunk was placed in my hand as the celebrant said, "The body of Christ, the bread of life." Dipping it in the sweet-smelling wine, I heard the words "The blood of Christ, the cup of salvation." The experience of the Eucharist came alive because my senses were heightened. The aroma transformed the Communion experience into an embodied encounter with Christ.

○ *Aromatherapy:* From scented candles to fragrant oils, the practice of aromatherapy deepens prayer for many people. Experiment with aromas that lead you more deeply into relaxation and open you to the Spirit. Add some lavender to your bath and sink into the warm water, "soaking up" the comfort and love of God.

With every breath we take, we engage our sense of smell. As we pay attention to the constancy and reliability of the breath, this keen sense can deepen our prayer.

TASTE

A friend invites us over to dinner. The notice for a church event invites, "Bring a covered dish to share." Someone experiences a loss, and we take food to express support; a celebratory meal at a special restaurant makes a birthday memorable; family bonding occurs around the dinner table. Our ability to taste adds Life to our life, and the body knows this instinctively. When we anticipate favorite foods, our salivary glands swing into action without our direction.

○ *Grace:* Our spirits respond to taste too. Grace before meals, a hallowed ritual for Christians, reminds us that God is the source of all abundance, not only the bounty before us but also the capacity to taste and digest it.

○ *Silent Meals:* Sense of taste is heightened when we eat in silence. At a silent retreat recently, the discomfort was obvious as twenty of us dined together without words, without social contact. After a while, however, as we became more familiar with the practice, our focus on the taste and texture of the food became more acute. We ate more slowly and deliberately; we relished each bite with prayerful attention and gratitude.

○ *Tasting Prayer:* As you repeat the words or sing "Taste and see that the Lord is good," enumerate specific aspects of your life that reflect the goodness of God. They don't necessarily have to be sources of pleasure; they could be painful occasions when you felt supported by friends or immersed in God's presence.

PRAYER OF DISTRACTION

It seems appropriate to include an honest prayer of frustration when nothing seems to be working. Any visit to the Psalms reminds us that God can handle—and perhaps even cherishes—our honest expressions.

Gracious God, it seems that what most holds my attention are those things and people that I can see, touch, hear, and feel. Yet, in the moments of my day when my mind is still, my soul is quiet, and my breath is slow and even, I can almost detect a whiff of your presence.

These precious times are all too fleeting; they slip away almost as quickly as they come. The phone rings, my child cries, a colleague needs my assistance, or my mind just simply gets distracted.

Help me know, O God, that you are still present with me, even in my distractions and interruptions. But also help me savor those spiritually centered moments so much that I will make room in my life for more of them.

When I am impatient because I can't see, touch, hear, or feel you, let your love seep surely into me until my heart turns back to you in surprise and delight. Amen.

Whether you're feeling the warmth of a cozy fire or biting into a delicious piece of chocolate, the celebration of the senses can be a potent reminder that we are indeed "fearfully and wonderfully made." Our capacity to see, hear, touch, smell, and taste can energize our prayer lives by opening new channels in our relationship with our Creator.

FOR REFLECTION

1. Which of your five senses seems most acute, more highly developed and sensitive than the others?
2. How can you use that natural connection with the world in choosing a prayer practice?
3. Which of your senses seems the least acute?
4. Select or create a practice that will develop this part of you.
5. Go through the list of senses once more; use your imagination to create a prayer practice to add to the list provided in the chapter.

5

PRAYING WITH THE SILENCE

*Now there was a great wind, so strong that it was splitting mountains
and breaking rocks in pieces before the* Lord*, but the* Lord *was
not in the wind; and after the wind an earthquake, but the* Lord
*was not in the earthquake; and after the earthquake a fire, but the
Lord was not in the fire; and after the fire a sound of sheer silence.
When Elijah heard it, he wrapped his face in his mantle and went out
and stood at the entrance of the cave. Then there came a voice to
him that said, "What are you doing here, Elijah?"*

1 KINGS 19:11-13

Be still, and know that I am God!

PSALM 46:10

For God alone my soul waits in silence.

PSALM 62:5

S eekers typically relate their first experience with the practice of
silence differently. I remember sharing a knowing laugh with a
friend as he described the discomfort of his initial silent retreat.

"Quiet? Are you kidding? As soon as the noises stopped, all these little
people inside me began to talk all at the same time!" He had anticipated
inner serenity, but what he got was inner chaos.

It's no wonder that the interior voices we have shushed for years fill the
silence with their impatient cries. However, if we can be still long enough
to give them a decent hearing, we finally may be introduced to what Jesus

referred to as "the kingdom . . . within" (Luke 17:21, NIV), the soul's center where the still, small voice of God can be heard. These "voices" are sometimes brazenly honest, revealing inner criticism, self-doubt, old resentments, and persistent questions, as well as buried dreams, sacred wisdom, and holy comfort. What inner promptings enter your own stillness?

Scripture tells us that as we open our hearts to the love of God, the words of Jesus can be trusted: "we will come to them and make our home with them" (John 14:23). Our part of the promise is to open the door and welcome their entry into our inner sanctum. But how can we discover this kingdom within if we never *go* there?

We usually try to talk our way into the kingdom rather than entering the uncertainty and waiting. Don't get me wrong, I love words—the sight of them on the page, the vibration of them in the air, the delicious feel of them as they roll out of my mouth, their power to describe and delight. Come to think of it, I love *water* too, but I try not to forget that I can drown in it as well as swim in it. Most of us are drowning in words.

We can become so enthralled with words that we begin to mistake the "right words" for the reality. For instance, we forget that reading a great book about prayer is not the same as praying. Words can become an end in themselves rather than a means that leads us to the experience of God. On the inner journey of spiritual formation, words can point to God but should not be mistaken for the experience of God. In the wise words of Barbara Brown Taylor, "Who wants to study a menu when you can eat a meal?"[1]

Our experiences of God are as varied as our faces, but there is one divine language that enriches the growth of introverts and extroverts alike—the language of silence. The sound of silence can be deafening and disturbing. It can feel like a colossal waste of time. I used to harbor secret judgmental feelings about its practitioners. After all, I reasoned, why sit mute and motionless when you could be feeding the homeless or healing the sick or doing something productive, for goodness' sake? At best, I considered silent practice as one of many forms of prayer, a mere appetizer on the rich buffet of spiritual options to partake of—or not. Silence had to change my life before I could change my mind.

Offering myself as an empty, though willing, container was the toughest discipline I ever tried. Since I am an extrovert, silent practice went against the grain of my personality. Yet seekers through the centuries witnessed to silence as the "language of God," and I felt compelled to keep trying. Eventually my curiosity turned to dogged commitment, even though silence didn't come easily for me.

It still doesn't, but God provided many teachers and companions along the way who helped me as a struggling novice to begin to experience—not just "know about"—availability and emptiness. An extrovert feeds on the energy of group process and conversation, so I was drawn naturally to the instant feedback of stimulating discussion, affirming eye contact with others, and lively voices engaged in exchanging ideas.

In that first year of trying to practice silent prayer I could find no one to share my longings. Seeing my spiritual director once a month was just about it. Finally someone introduced me to the practice of Centering Prayer by thrusting the instructions into my hand. Rising every morning to follow the directions in solitude, I felt like a bumbling beginner, trying to get it right. My mind wandered; my extroverted ego was resisting for all it was worth. When I began to enter times of silence, I encountered voices all right, but they were strange *inner* voices, an unruly chorus that I came to recognize as the infamous "monkey mind," the part of us that leaps from thought to thought like a monkey swinging from tree to tree. To calm the chaos inside, I resorted to my usual solution to any problem: try harder. I would simply switch to effort-mode and go galloping down the path toward being a "better Christian."

It didn't work. It took quite a while before I realized the process was more about letting go than trying harder. I had to (gasp) let go of control of my spiritual growth, allowing God to till the soil of my soul without my interference. Truth be told, most of us begin the spiritual journey using our natural methods of unconscious control. We decide when and where to attend worship, what scriptures to read, for whom we shall pray, what inspiring speaker to listen to, and what books to read. We are accustomed to being in the driver's seat—making good decisions and directing the journey. However, befriending the silence is

- more about yielding than controlling,
- more about loosening than grasping,
- more about participating than directing,
- more about allowing than managing.

When we submit to emptiness and silence, we take our hands off the wheel and relinquish control to the Holy Spirit. You would expect we could enter that vulnerability with trust, but at first it feels tender and naked. We may feel stripped of all pretense and the protection of words. Our instant evaluations of time in silence are often scathing: we insist we have listened and haven't heard one single thing. But when we aren't busy controlling things, it is possible simply to become attentive—discovering our truest selves in the mystery of silence as we learn this special language of God.

And change begins to happen, ever so slowly and subtly. It's a bit like waiting for the grass to grow. A wise mentor once told me that the silence of God is not the silence of a graveyard but the silence of a garden growing. Everything may appear to be dead and lifeless when we stand in the midst of a winter garden, but elementary biology tells us that bustling activity is going on underground, where we can't see it or control it. Sitting in silence involves the kind of emptying, *kenosis*, that allows the spiritual soil of the soul to be tilled and readied for the divine planting of seeds. These seeds ultimately will yield the fruits of the Spirit in unexpected ways. When we come to believe and trust in this divine planting, silence becomes our friend rather than an enemy. We can trust the not knowing and embrace the uncertainty, leaving the growth to God's wisdom.

Silent prayer is an exercise in radical trust. Stated bluntly, did I believe the Holy Spirit was real or not? Was God capable of influencing my inner core without my expert direction or not? Was this business of "trusting God" a word game that I played at church or did I actually believe it?

Silent practice can be a lonely pursuit at first, but I promise you it's worth it. If I could have organized it as a project or gathered a group of other extroverts around me to conquer the silence, I would have done my usual thing: talked it to death, analyzed it, and bought a stack of books about it.

All I can say is please give it a try. Will you experience an onslaught of interrupting thoughts? Absolutely. Will it seem impossible to control your monkey mind? To be sure. As you still your mind, voices inside your head compete for attention like hummingbirds on a holiday. Don't condemn; just notice with an inner smile. Don't evaluate; just leave the timing and the harvest to God. Enter the spacious freedom found in radical trust, the freedom that doesn't have to know what's happening or when or how.

Try the following prayer disciplines to ease yourself into silent practice.

CENTERING PRAYER

Most practitioners of Centering Prayer begin with Father Thomas Keating's book *Open Mind, Open Heart.* The organization Contemplative Outreach, a network of individuals and faith groups committed to the contemplative life, has trained hundreds of teachers in Centering Prayer. They in turn have introduced other Christians to this life-changing discipline. Here are the basic guidelines:

1. Choose a sacred word as the symbol of your intention to consent to God's presence and action within. [Any word is acceptable: Peace, Joy, Open, Jesus, Lord, Abba, Yes—whatever seems appropriate to you. Don't change the word during the prayer; that

would engage the thinking process rather than the silence.]

2. Sitting comfortably and with eyes closed, settle briefly, and silently introduce the sacred word as the symbol of your consent. . . .

3. When you become aware of thoughts, return ever-so-gently to the sacred word.

4. At the end of the prayer period, remain in silence with eyes closed for a couple of minutes.[2]

Though prayer periods of twenty-minutes twice a day are recommended, even a five-minute commitment can begin the cultivation of this discipline. It embodies radical trust in the guidance of God more than any other practice I know. Let go of all evaluation and trust the work of the Holy Spirit. Further instructions are available in Keating's book and also from www.contemplativeoutreach.org, which will lead you to a Centering Prayer group in your area.

BE-STILL-AND-KNOW PRAYER

A verse of scripture provides the structure for this silent exercise. Sit quietly as you meditate on portions of the verse, allowing the words to speak to you. Take the familiar verse from Psalm 46:10 and pray it in five-minute segments for a total of thirty minutes.

- ○ Be still, and know that *I am God.* (Meditate prayerfully for five minutes. How do you experience the reality of God? In what ways does this phrase matter in your life?)
- ○ Be still, and know that *I am.* (Another five-minute pause. Consider the concept of God as the great I AM. Express gratitude for the grandeur of God, which is greater than we can fathom.)
- ○ Be still, and know that *I.* (Another five-minute pause. Get in touch with the deepest part of your soul, where your authentic self resides. Feel the uniqueness and reality of who you are. Be open to a deep encounter with the God who created your special self.)

❍ Be still, and *know*. (Five minutes. What does it mean to know God instead of just knowing *about* God?)

❍ Be *still*. (Five minutes. Breathe deeply, allowing your body to sink into relaxation on the exhale. Be open to the calming sacred Presence as you become still enough to receive it.)

❍ *Be*. (Five minutes. Realize that simply being who you were created to be is enough. Give thanks for this brief opportunity to focus on the presence of God in your life.)

SITTING IN SOLITUDE

In a quiet place where you can be alone and quiet, focus on one thing: a bird at the feeder, the ripples on a watery surface, the shape of a cloud, a favorite icon, a cross at the altar, even your own hand. Allow your breathing to become progressively slower and deeper until you relax to a pace that permits listening for God's guidance. Don't try to direct or manipulate your thoughts; simply allow yourself to be in God's presence, using the object you've selected to guide you into a sense of peace, a surprising insight, or wherever it might lead you.

TEACH ME TO BE SILENT

This historic prayer comes from sixteenth-century Germany.

> Teach me, O Holy One,
> > The silence of humility,
> > The silence of wisdom,
> > The silence of love,
> > The silence of perfection,
> > The silence that speaks without words,
> > The silence of faith.
> Teach me to silence my own heart that I may listen to the gentle movement of your Spirit within me and sense the depths that are of God.

PRAYER OF SILENT UNION

○ Sit with your back straight but relaxed. Quiet your mind with a few deep, relaxing breaths. Slightly lengthen the time of each exhale as your body feels more rooted to the seat. Center your awareness on the silent and infinite presence of God within your heart.

○ Let the Spirit lead you beyond the noisy world into the silent realm within you. There God dwells as the source of your being.

○ Continuing your breathing, center on that hushed point within you where the human touches the Divine, where the branch intersects with the Vine, where you and God are one.

○ Simply let your prayer evolve into a state of silently *being there* with the immensity of God.

○ Without any need for thoughts and images and words, exchange quiet love with God.

PRAYER FOR THE SILENCE

This prayer from the Celtic community of Iona, Scotland, powerfully underscores the importance of silent practice:

When the world tells us we
are what we do with
our activity, acumen, or achievement,
let us learn
WE ARE WHAT WE DO WITH OUR SILENCE.

When the world tells us
we are what we do with our spending power, selling power, or our
    power of speech, let us learn
WE ARE WHAT WE DO WITH OUR SILENCE.

When the world tells us
to drown the silent sufferings of others with indifference or noise

or to forget the art of stillness even in the storm,
let us learn
WE ARE WHAT WE DO WITH OUR SILENCE.

When the world tells us
to rush in where angels fear to tread,
let us learn that angels listen first
before they take a step
for the voice of God in the silence.[3]

PRAYER AFTER SILENT PRAYER

This anonymous prayer is a refreshing reminder to let go of all evaluation
of a prayer session, trusting God to work within, unseen and undirected.

My time of prayer is finished, trailing its ashes like an incense stick
burned to the end. Quiet my mind before it passes judgment on
this prayer, my gift to you.

How can I judge its worth—this struggle to still my mind in
you, my efforts to feel your presence in my prayer? Only you can
judge the simple song of love sung in the noisy chambers of my
heart, often drowned by the wail of fear or the sweaty shouts of
work that must be done.

You, my hidden God, waited in patience as memories called
from the past and future prospects clamored for attention, filling
my mind with yesterdays and tomorrows, stealing my sense of your
presence.

As I prepare to go about my work, may my intention to live in
your present moment be the pattern for this day and for my life.
With your help, may I forever do only one thing at a time—always
in communion with you, my God, with all my heart and mind and
soul. Amen.

Prayer practices such as these break down the resistance to silence. It
no longer feels like a waste of time or an arena for failure but more like
creating a space where we trust God to work with us. It is a receptive

mode of prayer in which loving God for God's Self becomes more important than achieving an outcome. Besides that, it underscores the difference between expectation and hope: expectation is linked to results, but hope leaves us open to God's surprises. Who knows? In time we might begin to regard the silence not as an enemy but as an intimate friend.

FOR REFLECTION

1. How have you felt about silent practice in your prayer life up until now? Have you considered it a waste of time? a practice for introverts or saints? a scary place of too little control? Or is it already a part of your spiritual life? If so, what role does it play?

2. Would you be willing to commit as little as five minutes per day to open yourself to God in the silence? When and where would you engage this kind of prayer? If you practice silence in some way now, how might you deepen the practice?

3. Consider what would be your greatest barriers to the practice of silence. How might you approach the dismantling of these blocks?

4. How do you experience praying in silence as a matter of radical trust?

5. How do you think God might change you through this method?

6

PRAYING WITH THE SURROUNDINGS

Consider the lilies, how they grow: they neither toil nor spin; yet I tell you,
even Solomon in all his glory was not clothed like one of these.
LUKE 12:27

The heavens are telling the glory of God;
and the firmament proclaims his handiwork.
PSALM 19:1

W hat's around us affects what's inside us, and vice versa. I've known that in my head for a long time, but I have to learn it over and over again in my experience. During writing sessions, I repeatedly bumped up against a block that was difficult to diagnose: a frustrating difference between words penned on my sun porch and those written from my computer chair. In fact, every time I walked into my office space, I felt constricted, unimaginative, dull. I didn't have a clue what to do about it.

I consulted friends with special sensitivity to surroundings and decor, those who wouldn't ridicule my lack of creativity. My computer desk, they pointed out, positioned me facing the wall instead of the windows. Unfortunately, the crazy wiring in my one-hundred-year-old apartment made it impossible to change the placement.

However, I could change the appearance of the wall and what I would see around me when I was seated at my desk. So first the tan walls were painted green, the color of growth. In my field of vision as I sat at the computer, I hung my first feeble effort at watercolor painting on the wall to remind me that anything is possible. Mementos and newspaper clippings from long-past theater experiences reminded me that it's never too late to try something new. Certificates from courses and seminars evoked gratitude for teachers I had encountered through the years. But by far the most powerful change came from clearing the clutter.

Studies tell us that exterior clutter and interior confusion are bedfellows, and I believe it. We become so accustomed to our surroundings that their effect on our psyches and spirits goes unnoticed.

My office space, though improved by color and visual interest on the wall, still was littered with books and papers covering every cabinet and countertop. The renovation began. Boxes of theology books were hauled to a church that was rebuilding its library after a fire; paperback novels went to a local book drive; heavy art books went to the city library. Papers were filed, and paper clips slipped out of sight into drawers. The final magic touch was a narcissus plant—a gift from a friend—planted in gravel and laden with tight unopened buds of potential. I placed it directly behind the computer screen so that its fragrance and speedy blossoming would form a backdrop for the writing days. I hoped the blooming plant also would prompt a prayer for inspiration and creativity, which seemed more accessible on the porch with a view of the trees. And indeed, the narcissus helped.

Making the most of our surroundings usually requires us to slow down. Many of us move through life at a sprint, not a stroll. With upper body tilted ahead, we put our feet in fast-forward mode rather than pacing ourselves with the present moment. In this chapter, we'll explore prayers that remind us to notice where our feet are planted and look around for prayer prompts in our surroundings.

At a recent prayer retreat, the leader asked participants to reflect on times when we felt close to God. It didn't take me long to realize that in my personal life, almost all those pivotal spiritual moments had something in common. In each instance I had been alone and in a natural setting of some sort—in the desert, at the seashore, in the woods, sitting on a riverbank. Clearly, nature served as a religious icon in my experience.

The usual definition of a spiritual icon is a symbol or image, painted in the tradition of the Eastern Orthodox churches. Seen in a broader context, an icon is that which opens us up to the sacred, leads us through a portal to the holy. The centuries-old practice of praying with icons historically has led religious people more deeply into prayer. Being in the midst of God's creation can also serve this purpose, whether we are hiking a mountaintop or sitting in a rocking chair gazing at it.

Nature contains a well of images that never runs dry. The ocean's tide reminds us of life's rhythmic ebb and flow. The rising sun is emblematic of an unseen hand at the helm of the universe. A pond or lake can coax us to renew our baptismal vows. A towering saguaro cactus carries the image of standing tall and straight, even when scarred by time. Here are some prayer practices that invite us to allow God to speak to us through the world around us.

PARABLE PRAYER

This exercise encourages you to look for meaning in a detail that catches your eye. Stroll along at a leisurely pace, focusing intently on your surroundings. Be open to whatever draws your attention. Moss growing on a jagged rock could suggest that even the hardest things in life can yield growth. A leaf fluttering down might prompt you to ask, *What do I need to let go of so that I can float more freely in God's Spirit?*

The eye-catching symbol may be human-made. A radio tower could prompt the question, *Am I tuned in to God's frequency?* Or you may be led to pray the lyrics of a hymn: "Come, thou Fount of every blessing, *tune my heart* to sing thy grace."

Try your best not to manage the process. Allow an object to call to you. Then patiently attend to it as long as you can, opening yourself to its message for you. The path of prayer is most powerful when it is unpredictable.

PRAYER OF PRESENCE

No matter how busy you are, you can practice a portable prayer while you zip through your daily round. Aim to make several five-second connections during the day with folks you encounter—the supermarket clerk, someone waiting in line next to you, the person you bump into getting on the elevator, someone who seems to be an unwelcome interruption. Be brave enough to establish eye contact, a look that says "I really see you. You are not a bloodless appendage to the cash register. You are not someone who is duty-bound to serve me. You are of value."

Stay present to each encounter with eye contact, a smile, your sincere presence. What you get back doesn't matter. You're offering a gift, not making a trade.

THE TEACHING OF THE TREES

Scripture teems with rich lessons found in tree imagery. From the tree of the knowledge of good and evil (Gen. 2:9) to the tree on which Jesus was crucified (Acts 5:30), trees capture our attention and preach their sermons. Here are two prayer practices that open us to their teaching:

1. Find a large tree you can stand under. Be aware of your feet solidly planted on the ground and then slowly look up through the leaves and branches. Be silent for several minutes, open to what the tree has to teach you.

○ You may sense the tree's deep rootedness, the source of its strength.

○ You may consider the way the tree shares life with its leaves or how it bears fruit or flowers.

○ You may notice the tree's wounds and knots, scars from the buffeting storms; let it tell you how it keeps growing in spite of it all.

○ You can learn from the tree's hospitality, as it offers shelter to birds and squirrels and provides shade to you at this moment.

2. Sit comfortably next to a sturdy tree—on the ground or on a bench or swing. Consider these words by writer Mark Nepo as he encourages us "to rest like a tree" and learn the beauty of letting go, allowing everything to come and go like wind, without disturbing our rootedness.

> Like everyone, I'd rather not experience the undercurrents of life, but the challenge is not to shun them, but to accept that over a lifetime we will have our share of them.
>
> Avoiding the difficult aspects of living only stunts our fullness. When we do this, we are like a tree that never fully opens to the sky. And dwelling on our difficulties only prevents them from going on their way. When we do this, we are like a great tree that nets the storm in its leaves.
>
> The storm by its nature wants to move on, and the tree's grace is that it has no hands. Our blessing and curse is to learn and relearn when to reach and hold, and when to *put our hands in our pockets.* (emphasis added)[1]

SACRED SPACE

Do you have a prayer corner, a designated spot for reflection and meditation, or a personal altar? Creating your own inspirational environment enables you to participate in a pathway to prayer.

Collect objects that hold special significance for you—a candle, seashell, rock, plant, framed icon, or photo—whatever invites you into communion with the Holy. Place the objects on a table or windowsill and allow them to lead you into prayer. Change the items often so that the space doesn't become humdrum.

At this very moment, the narcissus plant positioned behind my computer is bursting with blooms that remind me to "consider the lilies, how they grow" (Luke 12:27). As I try to complete this chapter, I want to emulate those lilies Jesus talks about. They simply turned to the light of the sun, being what they were created to be—not zinnias, not marigolds but lilies. I too now pause and turn my face to the Light in patient waiting.

FOR REFLECTION

1. Think through one of your average days—where you go, what you see, what you do. Choose one object in your surroundings that could become a reminder to pray. How could that symbol become a means of grace?

2. Examine ways you relate to strangers who cross your path. How might these chance encounters prompt you to pray?

3. Take a good look at your work and home environments. How do you feel when you enter these rooms—nurtured or anxious?

4. What could be removed, added, or changed to create more harmonious or prayerful spaces?

7

PRAYING WITH THE CIRCUMSTANCES

Give thanks in all circumstances.
1 THESSALONIANS 5:18

I was doing it again. The old pattern had returned—dressed in different circumstances. I sat in the beautiful Orpheum Theatre, waiting for the matinee to begin. Eager to see a famous musical, I had blown my budget on an expensive ticket in the center of the tenth row. But before the orchestra could even strike up the overture, I was scoping out the nearest exit. Was it the fastest route to the parking lot? If I scurried out during the curtain calls, maybe I could beat the crowd and get home in time to put a pizza in the oven before *60 Minutes* started. Why didn't I have the foresight to get an aisle seat for a quicker getaway? In other words, I was living on top of the familiar free-floating anxiety of "hurry up." It was a state of interior finger tapping. I was unable to be present because I was already invested in the next thing, however trivial that might be.

This feeling of distraction triggered a sense of déjà vu. I definitely had been here before. In fact, during the previous week I had been at fault in a fender bender because I was thinking about my destination instead of paying attention to the details of driving. On most days, by 3:00 PM I would be slightly behind schedule, reprimanding myself for not completing my to-do list. Clearly I needed to address this hurry habit. Again.

Years of good intentions—even fervent prayers of "Dear God, help me to be more present"—had yielded few permanent results. Was I sabotaging my own growth? How was I getting in the way? With uncharacteristic patience, I held the prayer on my heart for the next few days: "Show me how to deal with this dreadful condition of the need to hurry up—this feeling of being constantly behind the eight ball." Clearly I was called to pray about this habit in a new way.

As I tried to remain in a watch-and-pray mode, a strange statement kept returning to my mind and appearing on the pages of my journal: "You're programming your own frustration." That sentence chased me like a relentless pursuer until finally I had to turn around and face it. I had to take responsibility for my part in the habit, the cloudy outcome of free will and personal choice. God was not about to fix my circumstances without my cooperation. I was being invited to participate in my own healing by shining the light on my behavior. And I wasn't looking forward to it.

So far, so good. I was ready to take an honest look in the mirror. However, I knew from past experience that *thinking* about it, *talking* about it, and *analyzing* it wouldn't change a thing. I needed to come up with a behavioral tool to help me *do something* about it. Sometimes it's not enough to say, "I'll try to do better." Some of us need a prayer tool for building a bridge to change, to cooperating with God's desire for our growth rather than impeding it. I hammered out the following practice as that tool. It's a prayer that works best for natural list-makers. Skip it with no guilt if it doesn't feel comfortable for you.

PREPARATION PRAYER

As you awaken, repeat the words of Psalm 118:24. Name the day, the month, and the year to drive home the fact that you are focusing on *today*.

> This is the day that the LORD has made;
> let us rejoice and be glad in it.

List (on paper) all activities/appointments to be accomplished that day. Include everything—even minor tasks, such as a trip to the grocery store, a dental appointment, cleaning out a closet, as well as work hours, and so forth.

1. Scrutinize the list to determine whether you've listed more items than time allows you to accomplish. Is there more to do than you have energy to do? Will you be running late because the schedule is too loaded?

2. If there are too many entries, start ruthlessly trimming the day's plans. Target activities that can be delegated, moved to another day, scheduled to a later month, or discarded altogether. Cross them off the list.

3. When the list has been reduced to a manageable size, rewrite the entries in chronological order to see the flow of the day ahead. Affirm that it has "margins" around it—that is, reasonable time for the inevitable interruptions or moments of relaxation.

4. Pray through the list. Imagine the Light of God surrounding each activity, as if the Spirit is going before you and beside you, empowering you with energy, focus, and purpose. *Inhale* each task mindfully and slowly; *exhale* the sense of urgency.

5. Affirm once again that "*this* is the day that the LORD has made; let us rejoice and be glad in it."

A treasured scripture story grounds me in this practice. Oddly enough, it's the story of the good Samaritan, found in Luke 10. When Jesus tells the tale of the unlucky traveler injured by robbers, he speaks of the priest and the Levite who "passed by on the other side" (v. 31) before the compassionate Samaritan rescues the victim. The priest and the Levite probably were on their way to do worthwhile things, perhaps even at the synagogue. They had things to do and places to go and important calendars to follow.

The Samaritan, on the other hand, had time to stop. He was totally present to the needs of his neighbor without the distraction of where he was going next.

When we are loyal to the present moment, we can be busy without being harried.

TRANSITION PRAYER

If you are looking for a sense of direction during a time of transition, this discipline can help you discover where God may be leading you through your gifts and graces. If you're puzzled about what lights your fire, you can glean a great deal of information by following this prayerful practice for a few weeks. Be sure to make your answers specific, not general. For instance, in answer to what made you smile, rather than observe, "Everyone was nice," you might note, "When my daughter said, 'I love you, Mommy' for no apparent reason." Make your answers simple, specific, and personal.

At the close of the day, reply to the following questions in a journal set aside for this purpose:

- What caused me to smile today?
- What touched or moved me to tears today?
- What inspired me today?
- What was "life-giving" to me today?
- What felt "life-taking" to me today?
- When did I feel a burst of energy today?
- What sparked my curiosity today?
- What was I doing when I lost track of time?
- What did I learn about God and myself today?

INTERCESSORY PRAYER

Certainly the circumstances that often enter our prayer life involve our concern for others. There's not a right or wrong way to pray for others; any sincere prayer of the heart seems valid to me.

My own practice of intercessory prayer has been changing over time. One day when I received a disturbing phone call about a friend's illness, I felt my heart twist. As I wrestled with the question in my head, *How shall I pray for her?* I felt as if God was saying, *You just did!* Maybe the quickening of compassion inside me *was* the prayer, and the actual words were for me, not God. In a mysterious holy process, God already had heard the prayer of my heart.

We pray more unspoken prayers than we realize. Truth be told, sometimes our words don't match the desire of our hearts. Perhaps we're mouthing sentiments that don't reflect our inner feelings honestly. Congruence between our intentions and prayers is vital. As Gandhi wisely reminded us: it's better to have a heart without words than words without a heart. Sometimes a sincere prayer for someone else involves putting legs on our prayer, taking the time to ask (or imagine) what this person truly needs. Instead of dropping off a casserole or a cake (so that we can check that off a to-do list), we might discover that assistance with housecleaning, a sack of disposable dinnerware, or someone to feed and house pets for a few days is the critical need.

I am praying more thy-will-be-done prayers. I've come to believe that I have no business telling God what ought to happen. Petition and intercession are valid, but there's a difference between asking out of our relationship with God and directing God on how to run things. Of course, when we are in distress, we naturally plead in anguish for God's help with specific requests. But I no longer need to figure out what I think will be best and then ask God to grant it. Surely the wisdom and providence of God exceed our own. As we pray for others, it's important to trust the mystery of prayer without judgment or evaluation and to be willing to be part of God's loving response. Intercessory prayer isn't about manipulating God's will; it's about placing ourselves and those for whom we pray in the loving Presence that never abandons us, no matter the circumstances.

HOSPITAL PRAYER

The hospital can be a lonely place. Whether we're occupying a bed or standing beside it, we're in an atmosphere of overwhelming need. Words, flowers, cards—all are forms of caring prayer. Hundreds of churches now have active prayer-shawl ministries that have brought tactile comfort to countless folks in the hospital. Those who wrap themselves in the warmth of the shawls literally feel the power of the prayers.

Here again, loving prayer focuses on what the sick person needs, not what we need. Does he need someone to make phone calls, do laundry, write thank-you notes? Is she exhausted by visits, or does she need someone to stay all day? We participate in the prayer by being a partner with God in ministry, a channel of divine love.

The next time you find yourself walking hospital corridors, imagine that the light of the Holy Spirit is shining on the path before you, behind you, and encircling the sick bed with the light and love of God. Awareness of that divine Presence can shape your words and deeds as you become a channel of the healing Presence in whatever situation you encounter.

WHAT'S HAPPENING PRAYER

Sandy was exasperated about her apparent lack of time for prayer. Her house was undergoing renovation, and new carpet was being installed. Dealing with a persistent back ailment made it difficult for her to get up and go before the workmen arrived, so her morning devotional routine was sabotaged.

Spiritually speaking, her relationship with God was undergoing renovation too. She was expanding her image of God, shifting from God as a stern judge constantly displeased with her efforts to a more accepting Presence who loved her no matter what. So, in our spiritual guidance sessions together, we explored the possibility of using what was actually happening in her circumstances as a discipline through which her soul could grow.

First of all, she had to sort through all her "stuff" and clear the room for the carpet installers. As mentioned earlier, studies show that exterior clutter affects interior clutter; chaos on the outside often produces confusion on the inside. Practicing simplicity in our environment can promote clarity of the soul and mind. Sandy prayed through the sorting process, giving thanks for the memories evoked by the objects and placing them in one of four containers: trash, keep, sell, donate.

Next, as the new carpet was laid, she looked forward to the new way of "walking" in her spiritual life, moving with more freedom, more risk, more willingness to make mistakes, more humor, more acceptance. The physical act of stepping on a new surface became a trigger to remind her of new life in Christ. Soon there was a spring in her step!

What's happening in your own life that can signal your soul to grow? Are you starting a new job? moving to a new house? Recall the encouraging words from Isaiah: "I am about to do a new thing; now it springs forth, do you not perceive it?" (Isa. 43:19). Breathe deeply and play with images from your own life that bring new dimensions to your relationship with God.

LISTENING AS PRAYER

During a session of the Academy for Spiritual Formation, writer Robert Benson made a statement that brought tears of truth to my eyes: *Sometimes being listened to is so much like being loved that it's impossible to tell the difference.*

I would add to that: listening is a powerful way to pray. Think of a time when someone listened to you intently without interruption, without fixing, without pointing out where you went astray or how you could get back on track, without describing how he or she would have handled similar circumstances. Listening is a gift of safety, acceptance, and prayerful presence.

"IT IS AS IT IS" PRAYER

One of the more difficult aspects of the spiritual life is balancing honesty and hope. Obviously, it is psychologically healthy to feel the pain when we have been injured inside or outside or our lives have been permanently altered. But when do we decide to move on? to discontinue our recitation of how wounded we are? to shift the energy from what happened to us to what we can do now? It's easier to stay wounded than to heal. No one can be healed for us. The healing must come *to* us *through* us.

This prayer invites us to stop our downward spiral of victim talk with a simple phrase to break the pattern: "It is as it is." We insert the phrase into our thoughts anytime we become aware that we are revisiting the negative thoughts. This practice can provide the impetus to shift from pain to possibility and plunge us right smack into the present moment. Yesterday's history can't be rewritten, but this prayer can at least open our hearts to tomorrow's hope.

Seen through the eyes of faith, challenging life circumstances can be a means of our growth rather than its saboteur. Whether we landed in the challenging circumstances through accident or ignorance, through another's folly or our own, we can rest on the bedrock truth of Romans 8:28: "All things work together for good." God can use anything and everything to shape us into the image of Christ. You can count on it.

FOR REFLECTION

1. What is the most challenging circumstance in your life right now? Can you see God's grace accompanying you, breaking through in the midst of difficulty? in spite of it?

2. What is the most delightful circumstance in your current experience? Is there an invitation to learn more precisely what gives you life?

3. How have you prayed for others in the past? Can you think of ways to broaden your concept and practice of intercessory prayer?

4. How is "praying with the circumstances" related to prayer as relationship rather than results?

Epilogue

PRAYING WITH YOUR LIFE

The LORD will guide you continually,
and satisfy your needs in parched places
. . . .
and you shall be like a watered garden.
—ISAIAH 58:11

I 've been dancing around this prayer thing as long as I can remember. There's always been a puzzled part of me that said, *Why? How? Who said so?* And that voice only became more persistent as I grew up. I wanted to understand prayer more clearly, but it became more mysterious as the years went by—not a comfortable situation for a young person in search of right answers.

In my late thirties my frustration became so insistent that I found myself in the office of a trusted pastor friend, pouring out my confusion. After I closed the door of his office behind me, I said defiantly, "Look, I have something important to ask you, and I won't betray your confidence if you'll just tell me the truth. No preacher talk, just the unvarnished truth." He hesitated, then motioned for me to take a seat.

The words came tumbling out: "I pray fervently for people to get well, and they die. I pray for marriages to be mended, and they end in divorce. I pray for peace in the Mideast, and violence escalates. Do any of the prayers really matter? Just tell me why *you* pray. No sugarcoating, OK?"

He slowly cleared his throat and uttered the words that have stayed with me from that day until this one. "When I feel the way you feel right now, Linda, I rest on this one thing. I pray *because Jesus prayed*. If I call myself a Christian, a disciple of Jesus Christ, that means I follow his lead. And, despite his own times of confusion and frustration, Jesus continued to pray and pray and pray." My pastor wasn't saying he understood prayer; he was saying he was committed to it.

We're not called to "get it right"; we're called to PRAY.

As a Christian, a follower of Christ, I've been living into his candid answer for more than thirty years now, paying attention in the Gospel stories about how and when Jesus prayed. He prayed in all circumstances—celebration times, times of heartache and disappointment, up times, down times, times of confidence, times of confusion—all of it. We're called to do the same, trusting that the same God who gives us the instinctual urge to pray is somehow hearing our prayers.

JESUS' RELATIONSHIP WITH GOD

We can take some clues from the Gospel descriptions of Jesus in prayer. Consider his perplexed prayer in the garden of Gethsemane, where he is described as "deeply distressed and troubled" (Mark 14:33, NIV). Scripture says that "he fell to the ground and prayed that if possible the hour might pass from him" (v. 35). In many other circumstances Jesus instinctively prayed, talking with Someone with whom he had a relationship of friendship and familiarity and irrational trust. It seemed to be a natural impulse, a conversation with someone close—so close that he spoke spontaneously and naturally. His "Abba" was a reality whose love he could trust even in bewilderment and fear. Jesus prayed in times of desperation and in times of delight. He prayed for healing; he prayed prayers of thanksgiving.

If this One at the center of our Christian story prayed in agony on the cross, in doubt in the garden of Gethsemane, and in triumph on the Mount of Transfiguration, then this attitude of infused prayer must be a vital part of our own Christian experience. Jesus prayed without ceasing because his relationship to God filled every fiber of his being and infused every moment of his days.

Sometimes I think we keep praying because in some profound way, we are shaped by offering ourselves. And we don't have to do it with lofty, pious language. We can be honest and real with the One who loves us and created us. Any tiny effort can be used. Prayer is the primary way in which we give God an opportunity to work with us.

Perhaps our prayer can be utterly candid: "Well, God, I'm not sure this is going to work, but I'll give it a try anyway. If you can do something with my pathetic stabs at prayer, then I'm willing!"

If prayer is about relationship rather than results, then it must be less about getting what we want and more about nurturing this amazing invitation to divine friendship. As human beings, we want to harness prayer—possess it and use it. Meaningful growth in prayer ceases to be a matter of what we can get from God but how we exist in God.

Pastor Steve Garnaas-Holmes illustrates this point as he comments on the familiar story of the prodigal son:

> There was a man who had two sons. The younger of them said to his father, "Father, give me the share of the property that will belong to me." . . . The older son said, "For all these years I have been working like a slave for you, and I have never disobeyed your command; yet you have never given me even a young goat so that I might celebrate with my friends." (from Luke 15)
>
> This is a story about two sons who are both selfish, and a father who is lavishly generous. As are all of Jesus' parables, it's a story about abundance. Notice that both of the sons treat the father the same: they do not care about him or his presence; they only want his stuff. Isn't that how we pray most of the time? We ask God for stuff: "Heal this disease. Make this work out OK. Answer my petition." But we don't simply open ourselves to God's presence. How seldom we pray, "God, no matter what happens, I just want to be with you." It comes from our fear that there won't be enough

blessing. When we feel that God does not answer our prayers, it's probably because we're just asking for God's stuff. But God's answer to our prayer is always the same: "You are always with me, and all that is mine is yours."

Even in praying for others we can pray our selfishness—"here's what I want"—and forget to pray our generosity: "Here's what I trust; here's what I offer." Christ invites us to be prodigal (recklessly extravagant) in prayer toward God and others, even those who have hurt us. This spirit of abundance is rooted in our most basic prayer: our openness to God's presence and blessing, and our desire to be present for the One who is present for us. It is to pray, "God, you are always with me, and all that is mine is yours."[1]

Every time I begin to question the reality of prayer, invariably an upsetting event will occur, and I feel (again!) that primal impulse to pray, an automatic reaching out to something greater, a reality "in whom I live and move and have my being" (see Acts 17:28). If that benevolent Source didn't exist, then why was I created to reach for it?

Prayer is not a category, not a compartment, but a connection. In other words, you can't put it in a box and declare, "I have it figured out now," because you can be sure that the mystery of prayer will continue to spill over the edges of any box we put it in. Part of growing up in our faith is growing up in prayer. And that involves our willingness to consider the boundless horizons of prayer.

The words *let your life be a prayer* form a lovely concept, one I've always been drawn to. But even as I write these words, I'm wondering how that actually looks in a flesh-and-blood person's life. How does it get lived out in the roller coaster of everyday existence?

PRAYING WITHOUT CEASING

"Pray without ceasing" has always seemed elusive as well. As a child encountering that bewildering Bible verse, I envisioned a monastic kind of nonstop mumbling, a literal speaking of words. But, thank goodness, growing up in body often prompts us to grow up in spirit, and, if we're open to spiritual formation, we begin to consider a broader concept of prayer. Frankly, it's hard to wrap our minds around what it may mean to have our lives become a prayer.

Those who have tried to explain this sacred process have come up with partial, limited definitions, and I'm no different. Each of us is attempting to describe a process or a reality that is beyond words. In the final analysis, seekers define unceasing prayer through a uniquely personal lens.

Here's what I see through my lens. Returning to the basic assumption that prayer is relationship rather than result, it is useful to ask ourselves, *What do we do when we live in close relationship with someone?* We're in that person's presence; we go about our daily tasks with awareness of and respect for him or her. We hang out together. We make time for each other. Conversation arises naturally as we share our concerns, our ups and downs. We try to be our authentic selves—no masks, no pretense—in a safe container of love and support. It's amazing that the God of the universe offers us this kind of kinship! Sometimes it seems as though we're like fish in the ocean, looking for water—searching urgently for the divine presence when we are swimming in it.

DANCING WITH GOD

God leads us to the awareness that prayer is not cordoned off in a separate space called "our spiritual life" but integrated into every moment of the day and every cell of our body. Literally everything is a part of our spiritual self—family life, church life, community life, social life. Existence becomes immersed in an attitude of prayer, not simply words of prayer.

The best metaphor I know for this constant state of prayerful guidance is a dance. Not just any dance, mind you, but a tango, an intimate movement in which the partners move in sync with each other, where the dance becomes instinctual. If you can imagine yourself as the female partner, each time the leading male partner shifts even slightly, you automatically follow. I think our dance with the Holy Spirit as our guide can be that integrated. Our own will becomes synchronized to the divine will. Of course, that close connection is the result of practice, trust, and abandonment to God's guidance.

Consider the words of this meditation on such guidance:

> When I meditated on the word Guidance, I kept seeing "dance" at
> the end of the word.
> I remember reading that doing God's will is a lot like dancing.
> When two people try to lead, nothing feels right.
> The movement doesn't flow with the music,
> and everything is quite uncomfortable and jerky.
> When one person realizes that, and lets the other lead,
> both bodies begin to flow with the music.
> It's as if two become one body, moving beautifully.
> The dance takes surrender, willingness,
> and attentiveness from one person
> and gentle guidance and skill from the other.
> My eyes drew back to the word Guidance.
> When I saw "G" I thought of God, followed by "u" and "i. "
> "God," "u" and "i" dance.
> God, you, and I dance.[2]

So why pray? There are many mysterious reasons.

○ Because Jesus prayed? Yes.

○ Because we're created with a desire to pray? Yes.

○ Because it's our entryway into the heart of God? Yes.

○ Because it allows God to show us who we are? Yes.

○ Because it leads us to participate in God's will for the world? Yes.

○ Because our lives are shaped by the praying? Yes.

○ Because it connects us to a Love greater than our own? Yes.

Yes. Yes. Yes!

As we dance with the Spirit, we can more nearly recognize the image of God placed within each of us, and we connect with that divine gift, God's very seed planted in our hearts and influencing every move we make and every thought we think. This intimate relationship leads us into new and exciting territory, an ever-expanding view of who God is, who we are, and how boundless the communication of prayer can be.

In other words, as we pray with our lives, with everything that we are, we can enter that place of freedom and abandonment to God—even in the messiness of life.

FOR REFLECTION

1. Take a careful look at your life as it is right now. Review the many prayer practices in this book. Can you commit to three specific forms of integrated prayer to make you more present to the Presence?
2. When and how will you incorporate these practices into your life as it exists?
3. What barriers are you likely to encounter as you broaden your practice of prayer?
4. Share your commitment with a trusted friend or a covenant group.

Appendix

GUIDELINES FOR GROUP USE

The content of this book can be adapted to a number of settings: covenant groups, home study groups, midweek fellowship groups, or church-school classes. Following is a sample format for a 1½-hour session. Choose supplemental elements from the list of hymns, opening and closing prayers, and additional discussion questions to suit the needs of your particular group, setting, and time allotment. Some suggestions refer to prayers printed in the text.

For the group sessions, each participant will need a copy of *Praying in the Messiness of Life*, a name tag, writing paper, and pen or pencil. Use the schedule below for Session 1 as the pattern for all subsequent meetings, selecting prayers and hymns of your choice. Choose among the reflection questions at the end of each chapter and the additional discussion questions and options offered here.

SESSION 1: BREAKING OUT OF THE PRAYER BOX

Opening and Introductions

At each session the leader welcomes the group and slowly reads aloud the scripture that opens the chapter for the week.

Opening prayer in unison: Prayer for an Open Heart (see page 103).

For introductions, have each person say his or her name and respond briefly to this question: *What is your earliest memory or impression of prayer?*

This question provides an entry into personal sharing and helps the group to begin focusing on the subject of prayer.

(Optional) Hymn "This Is a Day of New Beginnings" (No. 383, United Methodist Hymnal)

Discussion Questions

Share as a group or in small units of two to eight people.

○ How would you describe your own inner urge to embark on this prayer study? a need to expand your concept of prayer? a dryness or boredom in your prayer life? a vague spiritual restlessness? something else?

○ Discuss this statement: Prayer is more about relationship than results.

○ How would following this concept change your prayer life?

If time permits, review the questions at the end of the introduction.

Prayer Concerns

Invite participants to share prayer concerns as they wish so that they can pray for one another between meetings.

Closing Prayer: Sending Forth Prayer (page 104).

SESSION 2: PRAYING WITH THE BODY

Take a walk, using one of the walking meditations in the text. An outdoor stroll is ideal. If that isn't possible, improvise: walk around a room or sanctuary.

Pose these questions to the group and let participants share their responses as they are led.

○ How does your body feel when you hear something that seems true to you, something with which your soul resonates?

○ How does your body feel when you hear something that seems false?

○ Consider your relationship with your body. Do you experience your body as the "temple of the Holy Spirit"? Do you experience it as your friend or your enemy?

○ How might you be a "nurturing parent" to your own body?

Close with the prayer in the Hands section of chapter 1 (page 32) and/or Sending Forth Prayer (page 104).

SESSION 3: PRAYING WITH THE BREATH

Discuss the difference between a reaction and a response. Cite personal examples of each.

Practice abdominal breathing, either sitting or lying on the floor, as described in this chapter. As the leader reads the instructions, let this be a time of group silent practice.

Invite participants to share responses to these questions:

○ What are your most frequent triggers for irritation and impatience?

○ What gives you a surge of delight? a rush of adrenaline?

SESSION 4: PRAYING WITH THE MIND

Using the outline for *lectio divina* (page 47), lead the group in contemplating Philippians 4:8.

Ask members of the group to think of specific ways they habitually "feed the negative wolf." By complaining? gossiping? passing judgment? other means? Share with one another as people are comfortable doing so.

Then have people identify specific ways that they habitually "feed the positive wolf." By affirming others and oneself? smiling? shifting to thoughts of gratitude? Take time to share.

SESSION 5: PRAYING WITH THE SENSES

Structure this session around direct experience of the five senses: take the "Stroll for Your Soul" outside if possible, or choose an indoor location, perhaps a chapel or church sanctuary.

- ○ SEE: Provide an icon, painting, or print for a brief period of contemplation and place it in front of the group.

    Provide printed mandalas for participants with crayons, markers, or paints. Go to Web sites with free downloads, such as www.coloring castle.com/mandala_coloring_pages.html

    If you have a copy of the book *Praying With Color*, explain the simple method and allow time for each person to "pray a prayer with color."

- ○ HEAR: Play a piece of music (for example, "Hallelujah Chorus," "Old Rugged Cross," "Jesus Loves Me," "Lord, Prepare Me to Be a Sanctuary") and share reactions. What memories does the music uncover? How did it shape your theology?

- ○ TOUCH: Have the group sit in a circle. Go around the circle, beginning with the leader, and clasp the hand of the person next to you, slowly saying "God bless you, *name of person*." Each person blesses the next person in turn until each person has experienced the power of a loving touch.

- ○ SMELL: Pass around the circle a fragrant candle or flower (cinnamon, tuberose, pine, lily, for example). Share any associations or memories the scent evokes.

- ○ TASTE: After repeating the psalm verse "O taste and see that the LORD is good," share a meal, snack, or simply a piece of chocolate or a cookie.

SESSION 6: PRAYING WITH THE SILENCE

Review the process of Centering Prayer. Ask if any in the group have practiced this method; if so, they might speak briefly about it. Practice at least five minutes of group centering. Find out whether there are Centering Prayer groups in your area in case people would like to visit one.

After Centering Prayer, consider these questions:

○ When you are silent, what kinds of thoughts enter your stillness?
○ In what way do you think this statement is true:

Silence is the language of God.

If time permits, experience the Be-Still-and-Know Prayer (pages 66–67).

SESSION 7: PRAYING WITH THE SURROUNDINGS

Allow at least 15 minutes for participants to experience one of the "The Teaching of the Trees" suggestions (pages 74–75). Go outside, if possible. Otherwise, sit with eyes closed, imagining oneself beside a tree. Journal or share insights.

Divide into groups of two or three people and discuss these questions:

○ What effect does your home environment have on your connection to the Spirit?
○ How does clutter affect you? What about color? What simple changes could you make to enrich your personal space?
○ In what natural setting do you feel most connected to God?

SESSION 8: PRAYING WITH THE CIRCUMSTANCES

- Begin with a discussion of intercessory prayer. Share with one another experiences and suggestions about how to pray for others in a meaningful way. How does one decide on the action that follows praying?
- How do you put "legs" on your prayer?
- What is a current situation in your life that can be a metaphor to prompt your prayer?
- Describe an experience when mere listening felt prayerful for you. How does the response differ if you are the listener or the one listened to?

SESSION 9: PRAYING WITH YOUR LIFE

Discuss the statement "I pray because Jesus prayed." Share insights as you think through the Gospel accounts of Jesus' life of prayer. Then consider these questions in small groups:

- How have you dealt with your own doubts about the efficacy of prayer?
- Review the reasons to pray on page 92. How have you experienced these truths in your life?

Close your study with a ceremony of commitment and a celebration of Holy Communion if possible. Schedule a time of silent reflection during which participants may choose new prayer practices to broaden their life of prayer. They may write out their commitment and place it on the altar to signify their intention.

WEEKEND RETREAT

This material lends itself to a setting with outdoor access for reflection, walking exercises, and enrichment through nature. The following schedule may be adapted to your needs.

During each one-hour session, provide a brief presentation of the material, then use the remaining time for experiential activities. Encourage the group to choose one of the practices to engage individually. Or divide a large group into smaller clusters to discuss the questions at the end of each chapter, as well as the additional reflections in the appendix, if time permits.

Friday Night

5:00	Check-in
6:00	Dinner
7:00	Introductions, announcements, and overview of the weekend
7:30	Session 1 Preface and Introduction, Breaking Out of the Prayer Box
8:00	Group discussions and Prayer Experience
9:00	Evening Prayer

Saturday

8:00	Breakfast
9:00	Session 2 Praying with the Body; Praying with the Breath
10:15	Break
10:30	Session 3 Praying with the Mind; Praying with the Senses
Noon	Lunch
1:00	Free time (rest, exercise, games, walking meditations, reflection)
3:00	Session 4 Praying with the Silence
4:00	Break
4:30	Session 5 Praying with the Surroundings; Praying with the Circumstances

6:00   Supper
Evening Fellowship, games, movies, optional activities

Sunday
8:00   Breakfast
9:00   Session 6 Praying with Your Life
10:00   Break, Pack up
10:30   Worship with commitment (participants could commit to
            one or more new prayer practices, writing their intention
            on a slip of paper and placing it on the altar).
Noon   Lunch; Dismissal

NINE-WEEK STUDY

For this time frame, a group would read one chapter each week in preparation for the group session. Participants should be encouraged to try at least one of the prayer suggestions during the week so that they can share their experiences. Use the reflection questions as the basis for further discussion.

FIVE-WEEK STUDY

The introduction and chapter 1 would be assigned for the first week. During the following four weeks, the group should cover two chapters each week.

PRIVATE RETREAT

Read each chapter slowly, answering the questions at the end of sections in a leisurely and prayerful manner (recording your thoughts in a journal, if possible). Experiment with at least one prayer practice suggested in the chapter. Pace yourself according to the amount of time you have to cover the material. Don't neglect the prayer experience in order to complete reading the information. Remember: any practice is not an end in itself but a pathway to the experience of God.

PRAYERS FOR OPENINGS AND CLOSINGS

Prayer for an Open Heart

Loving God, we fling open the door of our hearts, releasing preconceived notions, old habits, and outworn ideas . . . making room for your guidance.

We let go of resentments, judgments, and envy to allow your healing love to cleanse us.

So we come to you today eager to grow, to burst through our narrow concepts of who you are and to discover who we are as your sons and daughters. We long to experience the wonder of your ongoing revelation and to become channels of your love and grace in this world.

We trust that your Presence is with us on this exciting journey to deeper prayer and heartfelt connection with you.

In Christ we pray. Amen.

Hearing Your Voice

O God, we marvel at your many sacred Voices, your holy summons
    from every corner of our lives:
A pastel sunset
A chirping cardinal
A loved one's smile
A child in need
A stranger's silence
An inspiring word of scripture
May we sense your Presence threading its way through the whole
    fabric of our lives.

Open our eyes to new ways of seeing you.
Open our ears to your gentle call to growth.
Open our hearts to your Love that will not let us go.
Through Christ our Lord. Amen.

Sending Forth Prayer

Send us forth, O God, with
every breath a thanksgiving,
every thought wrapped in compassion,
every word filled with kindness, and
every deed a channel of Love.
Through your grace, may our lives become a prayer.
Amen.

Prayer of Trust

O Holy One, be with me in my uncertainty, my confusion.
I hardly know which way to turn, yet my heart in expectation turns
to you.
Somehow I know—I trust—that you honor my willingness, because
it's all I have right now.
Even if I make a misstep and stumble, I trust your gracious Spirit to
steer me back on the path.

So accept my feeble effort, my availability, my deep desire to serve
you.
I no longer ask for a vision of the whole journey, but simply for the
next step.
Shine your holy light on my path forward, and I will take that step
with your loving, forgiving Spirit ever at my side.
Amen.

For the Spirit of Truth

(Prayer from Kenya, No. 597, The United Methodist Hymnal)
From the cowardice that dares not face new truth,
From the laziness that is contented with half-truth,
From the arrogance that thinks it knows all truth,
Good Lord, deliver me.
Amen.

Prayer to Love as God Loves

O God of love and compassion, you know us better than we know
   ourselves,
our ups and downs,
our successes and failures,
our good intentions and our broken promises.
Yet you continue to love us with infinite patience, as a steadfast
   parent loves a wayward child. You pour grace on us whether we
   deserve it or not. We marvel at that kind of gift!
May we respond to your grace by pouring grace upon everyone we
   meet, whether they deserve it or not
May we give without expecting anything in return.
May we love others unconditionally as you love us.
May we see the world and every creature in it—ourselves included—
   through your eyes only.
We pray in the name of your son Jesus, who showed us the depth of
   your love.
Amen.

Wellspring Prayer

(Adapted from John 4:13-15)
O Divine Wellspring, source of life and life's end,
   In whom all the tributaries of life converge,
Take us down the well of our own life to the eternal spring within,
   From which all people of faith have drawn.
Water now our thirsty souls,
   Through story, symbol, and words we speak,

Through the silences we keep,
Through the bread we share,
Through all entrusted to our care.
As we draw deeply from the wellspring of your great kindness,
May our lives be a wellspring of mercy, justice, and peace.
Amen.

Prayer of Thanks

Just this once, O God, I'd like to come to you with no mention of problems, but simply to say "Thank you . . ."

For your forgiveness, when I fail to do the loving thing;
For the sheer joy of sleep, when I'm terribly tired;
For the silent strength of humility, when pride overtakes me;
For the justice of your laws, when people are cruel;
For the growing remedies to good health, when I am ill;
For the nurture of new knowledge, when I make a mistake;
For the simplicity of orderliness, when I face confusion;
For the joy of helping others, when I see people in need;
For the assurance that you have made a place for each of us,
    when I feel inadequate among my peers;
For the earthly evidences of your will, when I am trying to find out
    what life is all about;
For the reality of your world, when I stray too far into fantasy;
For the rightness of reason, when I panic too quickly;
For the fun that refreshes, when everything gets too serious;
For the renewal of moments of silence, when I am dizzy being
    busy in a bustling world;
For the confidence of friends, when loved ones do not understand;
For the healing love of family, when friends hurt me;
For your presence, when I am lonely;
And, above all, God, I thank you for the meaning and fullness you
    have given this world of yours.
In the name of Christ. Amen.

—Author Unknown

SUGGESTED HYMNS

(These numbers come from The United Methodist Hymnal, 1989)
"Breathe on Me, Breath of God" (420)
"He Leadeth Me: O Blessed Thought" (128)
"O Master Let Me Walk with Thee" (430)
"Now Thank We All Our God" (102)
"Lord of the Dance" (261)
"Blest Be the Tie That Binds" (557)
"Open My Eyes, That I May See" (454)
"Spirit of God, Descend upon My Heart" (500)
"Sweet, Sweet Spirit" (334)
"Spirit of the Living God" (393)
"This is a Day of New Beginnings" (383)

Notes

INTRODUCTION

1. Wendell Berry, *Standing by Words: Essays* (Berkeley CA: Counterpoint Press, 1983), 97.
2. Steve Garnaas-Holmes, "God Is Mindful," *Unfolding Light*, 9/21/2010. (E-newsletter at http://unfoldinglight.net. To receive daily e-mail, contact unfoldinglight@hotmail.com.)

PRAYING WITH THE BREATH

1. Steve Garnaas-Holmes, "Breathing Compassion," *Unfolding Light*, 6/1/2009 (E-newsletter at http://unfoldinglight.net).

PRAYING WITH THE MIND

1. Linda Douty, "How Can I See the Light When It's So Dark?" *Journey to a Thankful Heart* (Harrisburg, PA: Morehouse Publishing, 2007), 66–67.
2. Marjorie J. Thompson, *Soul Feast: An Invitation to the Christian Spiritual Life* (1995; Louisville, KY: Westminster John Knox Press, 2005), 25–26.
3. Brother Lawrence, *The Practice of the Presence of God* (New Kensington PA: Whitaker House, 1982).
4. Steve Garnaas-Holmes, "Mindful Walk," *Unfolding Light*, 9/21/2007.

PRAYING WITH THE SENSES

1. Sybil MacBeth, *Praying in Color: Drawing a New Path to God* (Brewster, MA: Paraclete Press, 2007).

PRAYING WITH THE SILENCE

1. Barbara Brown Taylor, *An Altar in the World: A Geography of Faith* (New York: HarperOne, 2009), xvi.
2. Thomas Keating, *Open Mind, Open Heart* (Rockport, MA: Element Books, 1986), 139.
3. Kathy Galloway, ed., *The Pattern of Our Days: Worship in the Celtic Tradition from the Iona Community*, 2nd ed. (Mahwah, NJ: Paulist Press, 1999), 96–97.

PRAYING WITH THE SURROUNDINGS

1. Mark Nepo, *The Book of Awakening: Having the Life You Want by Being Present to the Life You Have* (York Beach, ME: Conari Press, 2000), 190.

EPILOGUE

1. Steve Garnaas-Holmes, "Prodigal Prayer," *Unfolding Light*, 3/10/2010.
2. "Dancing with God" © John Mark Ministries, jmm.aa.net.au/articles/16526.htm.